Helping Mothers to Breastfeed

Peg Marshall

Other AMREF Books

Helping Mothers to Breastfeed

Revised Edition

F. Savage King

Illustrated by

Sara Kionga-Kamau, Ivanson Kayaii, Helen Chown and Daphne Paley-Smith

AFRICAN MEDICAL AND RESEARCH FOUNDATION
1992

Published and printed by the African Medical and Research Foundation
Wilson Airport
P.O. Box 30125
Nairobi
Kenya

ISBN 9966–874–04–6

Please address any enquiries, suggestions or criticisms to:

Publishing Department
AMREF
P.O. Box 30125
Nairobi, Kenya

Contents

Foreword to the first edition

There is no doubt that breastfeeding is the best and safest way of feeding infants. It provides the only perfect food for babies, it protects them against infection, and it lays the foundation of their healthy psychological development. Kenya has recognized the value of this important and natural way of feeding babies. In recent years many activities have been directed at investigating infant feeding, and at publicizing the importance of breastmilk. The Kenya Code for Marketing of Breastmilk Substitutes aims to limit the promotion of formula. It should protect mothers from commercial influences which might tempt them to think that there is something better than their own milk for their baby.

There is still much to be done, however, to halt the spread of bottle and formula feeding that continues in both towns and rural areas, and to protect the precious custom of breastfeeding that is still, for most of our babies, the normal way to feed. The most urgent need, at this stage, is to improve the training of health workers in the art of helping mothers to breastfeed. Although health workers in Kenya generally favour breastfeeding, many do not know what they should do to help mothers to succeed.

In a country like Kenya, faced with a high population growth rate and very low contraceptive use, the promotion and protection of breastfeeding can help to reduce fertility. The frequency and duration of suckling determines the level of prolactin in the blood, the duration of ovarian suppression and, consequently, the length of lactational amenorrhoea.

This short book summarizes the most up-to-date ideas about breastfeeding and we hope that it will provide health workers in Kenya with the knowledge that they need to achieve what they really believe to be best. We in the Ministry are confident that this will be a major contribution to the health of our children, now and in the future.

Dr. W. Koinange, M.B.S.
Director of Medical Services
Ministry of Health
Nairobi

Preface to the first edition

This manual has been written at the recommendation of the Kenya National Workshop on Infant Feeding Practices which was held in Nyeri from 12–15 April, 1983. At that workshop, attention was drawn to the changes in infant feeding practices that are occurring in Kenya. The majority of women still breastfeed, and over 90% initiate lactation. However, an increasing number of women change to artificial feeding after a few weeks, or give bottle feeds, or some other supplement, in addition to breastfeeding, from too early an age.

The desirability of exclusive breastfeeding for 4–6 months has been widely promoted, and probably the majority of people recognize that it really is the best way to feed infants. A recent important study of the knowledge, attitudes, and practices about breastfeeding among health workers in Kenya, showed that they have a generally positive attitude. However, their knowledge of the mechanism of lactation, and of the practices and techniques that are necessary to help mothers to succeed, is limited. Consequently health workers and health institutions have a negative influence on breastfeeding because they continue to follow outdated practices.

New knowledge is now available about the factors that influence how mothers feed their babies, and the Workshop expressed concern that the ideas are not being used. One reason is that the information is not written down in a way that is accessible to those who need it.

This manual is written in an attempt to overcome this constraint. It is based partly on the book *Breastfeeding in Practice* by Elisabet Helsing and Felicity Savage King (OUP, 1982) which may be consulted for more detailed information. It also draws heavily on the experience and publications of the Breastfeeding Information Group (BIG) in Nairobi. Helping Mothers to Breastfeed is written for health workers in Kenya, and the group who have been responsible for monitoring its production hope that it fulfils most of their needs.

Dr. J. G. Kigondu
Dr. S. N. Kinoti
Ms. S. Nakissa
Ms. L. Kanaiya
Dr. F. Onyango
Dr. C.H. Wood
Dr. J. Bennett
Mrs. H. Armstrong
Dr. F. Savage King

Preface to the revised edition

This book has been widely used in Africa, and it has been translated into a number of other languages and adapted for a number of other cultural settings.

Since it was first published, knowledge has advanced, our understanding of how to help mothers has increased and considerable experience has been gained training health workers. Thus some revision has become necessary.

One of the most significant changes is the development of the section on breastfeeding and family planning to include the Lactational Amenorrhoea Method (LAM) of family planning.

Recently, concern with child spacing has become more urgent and the large number of potential pregnancies at present prevented by breastfeeding has been appreciated. If breastfeeding continues to decline, the need for family planning services will increase greatly, simply to keep population growth at its present level. At the same time, authorities have begun to realize the extent of the already unmet need for family planning services in many parts of the world.

The part that breastfeeding can play to enable a woman to control her own fertility has become clearer. Family planning should be available to all women, even when medical contraceptives are not. But many women and many health workers are confused about whether breastfeeding does or does not protect mothers against a new pregnancy, and about how reliable such protection can be. There is an urgent need for accurate information on this point so that women can choose how to space their children in the way that is most suitable for them, and can use their chosen method effectively.

The section on techniques of breastmilk expression has also been developed. Mothers of low birth weight or sick babies, and mothers who have to go out to work, need to be able to express their milk efficiently. Poor technique is a common cause of failure to use breastmilk optimally for these babies.

The section on nipple shields has been deleted as these appliances have been found to cause more problems than they solve. As health workers gain skill in helping mothers to position their babies correctly at the breast, the need for nipple shields anyway becomes less.

For much of the new material, credit must go to two colleagues from whom I have learned and continue to learn so much — Helen Armstrong and Chloe Fisher. But there are many others who have contributed, from all continents, including colleagues in IBFAN Africa, participants on training courses, and the many mothers whom I have met. I wish that I could name them all.

Felicity Savage King

Acknowledgements

Support for this project was provided by the Institute for International Studies in Natural Family Planning, Georgetown University, under Cooperative Agreement with the United States Agency for International Development (A.I.D.) (DPE-3040-A-00-5064-00). The views expressed by the authors do not necessarily reflect the views of A.I.D. or Georgetown University.

Publication of the Revised Edition has also been made possible by a generous grant from SIDA (Swedish International Development Authority) through TALC (Teaching-Aids At Low Cost).

CHAPTER ONE

Introduction

1.1 WHY MOTHERS NEED HELP

You may hear someone say: "Breastfeeding is natural—why should a woman need help?" Certainly some mothers are very lucky. They breastfeed their babies without any difficulty. But many women need help at the beginning—especially with their first baby, and especially if they are very young. Many women need help to continue breastfeeding, especially if they work away from home, or if the baby seems to cry a lot.

A study in Kenya* has shown that many women now use artificial feeds of one kind or another from an early age. These may be cow's milk, formula, diluted cereals, glucose water or plain water. The practice is commonest in the towns but it happens to some extent all over Kenya. In some areas it is traditional to give early supplements, especially if the baby cries. The majority of women continue to breastfeed partially at the same time, and this must prevent some of the worst effects of artificial feeding. But early supplements are an important cause of diarrhoea and breastfeeding failure. The result of their widespread unchecked use is likely to be that more and more women stop breastfeeding early.

If you ask women why they give up breastfeeding, or why they introduce supplements early, they give many different answers, such as:

---

* M. Veldhuis, J. K. Nyamwaya, M. W. Kinyua and A. A. J. Jansen, *Knowledge, Attitudes and Practices of Health Workers in Kenya with Respect to Breast Feeding*. Breastfeeding Information Group, Nairobi, 1982.

1

"I did not have enough milk", or, "The baby refused to suckle". However, though the women themselves do not know it, these are not the real causes of their difficulties. The women do not really lack milk. They may lack confidence that their milk is, by itself, enough for their baby. Sometimes the baby is not suckling in a good position. Some mothers lack enthusiasm to really try.

The underlying causes of their difficulties are:
- Lack of support from close female relatives.
- Delivering their baby in hospital.
- The pressures of modern urban life.

Lack of support from other women close to them

In traditional society, there were always experienced women nearby to help a new young mother. These might include her own mother, or the woman who helped her to deliver the baby. It would be someone that she knew and could trust. But in modern society, and especially in towns, there is often no helper nearby. Sometimes a woman's mother or mother-in-law is there to help, or she has other friends nearby, but they encourage her to give the baby artificial feeds, especially if they bottle fed their own children. Other family members too may encourage a woman to bottle feed, for example if they think that the baby cries too much.

Lack of support from health services

Delivering a baby in hospital may be safer for both mother and baby in many ways. But practices in many maternity hospitals make it more likely that mothers will introduce supplements, or give up breastfeeding completely, soon after they return home. Health workers in health centres and clinics often do not know how to support breastfeeding mothers, or how to help them with problems.

The pressures of modern urban life

There are many pressures on women to give their babies artificial feeds. For example: fashion; what their neighbours do; women's paid employment; public attitudes which make women feel uncomfortable breastfeeding in public; advertisements for formula; and the fact that it is so easy to buy breastmilk substitutes.

1.2 THE HELP THAT MOTHERS NEED TO BREASTFEED SUCCESSFULLY

Practical advice

A woman with her first baby may not be sure about how to put him to the breast. And the baby, although he can suck, may not take enough of the breast into his mouth. Mother and baby both need help to learn what to do. Putting the baby to the breast is very simple for a mother who knows how—but she has to know. If a baby does not take the breast correctly, it can cause many kinds of problem.

Women also want advice about how often to feed their babies, and about giving them other drinks and foods; about the common problems that they may have, such as sore nipples, sore breasts, not enough milk, too much milk, leaking breasts, and so on. New mothers need someone who knows what to do.

Psychological support

To breastfeed successfully, a woman must feel *confident*. This means:
- ❑ Believing that she can breastfeed. She must know that her milk is all that her baby needs and that her breasts, whatever their size or shape, will produce perfect milk in sufficient quantity.
- ❑ Knowing what changes to expect in her body. Then she understands that what she experiences is normal.
- ❑ Knowing something about how the baby will behave, and what she will have to do.

For the first weeks after childbirth, a woman is more sensitive and emotional than she was before. This helps her to love her baby, but also she easily becomes upset. She easily doubts her ability to look after her baby, and she easily does what other people tell her to do. If there is a small difficulty, or if someone asks her: "Do you really have enough milk?" she may be ready to stop breastfeeding altogether.

A new young mother needs a kind, experienced person to support her and to give her confidence. She needs to be "mothered" herself in her new role.

3

Close female relatives

A young woman's own mother, or other close female relatives, can give her confidence. If they are not nearby, someone else must support her. If relatives are encouraging a woman to bottle feed, she needs support to resist them.

Husbands

One of the best people to provide support is the woman's husband if he is available. He can help in many practical ways. Also he can tell her and other relatives that he wants her to breastfeed, and that he knows that her milk is the best food for their baby.

Figure 1. A husband can encourage his wife to breastfeed their baby.

Women's groups

Another valuable source of help is other women in the community, for example, breastfeeding counsellors, mother-to-mother support groups, or just friends who have breastfed. They may be particularly important to help women to continue breastfeeding after the first few months.

Support from health workers

The help and encouragement of health workers is essential, especially to start breastfeeding and to help with early problems. Health workers are in a key position, both in maternity wards and in health centres and clinics. They must give consistent, up-to-date advice, they must be kind and sympathetic, and they must reassure each mother that she certainly can breastfeed (see Chapter 11).

Health workers who do not do these things have a negative effect on breastfeeding, which makes failure more likely. Health workers who do give mothers help and support can make breastfeeding succeed. New research suggests that this is a very important factor.

CHAPTER TWO

The production of breastmilk and how a baby suckles

2.1 ANATOMY OF THE BREAST

The breast consists partly of gland tissue and partly of supporting tissue and fat. The gland tissue makes the milk, which then goes along small tubes or ducts towards the nipple. Before they reach the nipple, the ducts become much wider and form *lactiferous sinuses* in which milk collects. About 10–20 fine ducts lead from the lactiferous sinuses to the outside, through the tip of the nipple. The nipple contains many sensory nerves so it is very sensitive. This is important for the reflexes which help milk to come.

Around the nipple there is a circle of dark skin called the *areola*. On the areola you can see small swellings. These are glands that produce an oily fluid. The oil helps to keep the nipple skin soft and in good condition. Beneath the areola are the lactiferous sinuses.

2.2 THE MILK PRODUCING HORMONES AND REFLEXES

Milk is produced as a result of the action of *hormones* and *reflexes*. During pregnancy, hormone changes prepare the gland tissue to make milk. More gland tissue develops and the breasts become larger. Immediately after delivery, hormone changes make the breasts begin to produce milk. When the baby begins to suckle, two reflexes make the milk come in the right quantity and at the right time. You need to use your knowledge of the reflexes to help you advise a mother.

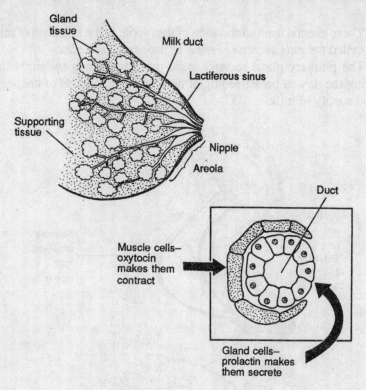

Figure 2. Anatomy of the breast.

2.3 PROLACTIN—THE MILK SECRETING HORMONE

The pituitary gland at the base of the brain produces a hormone called *prolactin*. Prolactin makes the gland cells in the breast secrete milk.

Every time the baby suckles at the breast he stimulates the nerve endings in the nipple. These nerves carry messages to the anterior part of the pituitary gland, which makes prolactin. The prolactin goes in the blood to the breasts and makes them secrete milk. Prolactin works after the baby suckles, and makes milk for the next feed.

The baby's suckling makes the breasts produce milk.

These events, from stimulation of the nipple to the secretion of milk, are called the *milk secreting reflex*, or the *prolactin reflex*.

The pituitary gland secretes more prolactin during the night than during the day so breastfeeding at night especially helps to keep up a good supply of milk.

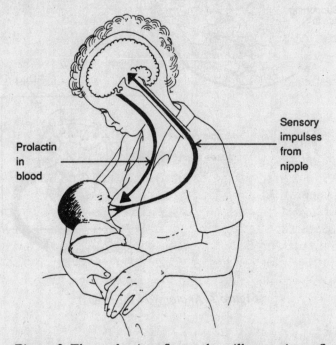

Prolactin
in
blood

Sensory
impulses
from
nipple

Figure 3. The prolactin reflex or the milk secretion reflex.

Supply and demand

It is very important to understand the effect of suckling on milk production. If the baby suckles more, the breasts make more milk. If the baby suckles less, the breasts make less milk. If the baby stops suckling completely, or if he never starts, the breasts stop making milk. If a mother has twins and they both suckle, then her breasts will make the extra milk that two babies need.

This is called *supply and demand*. The breasts supply as much milk as the baby demands. If a mother wishes to increase her milk supply, the best way to do it is to encourage the baby to suckle both longer and more often. She should *not* miss a feed to try to "save" her milk—that will make her breasts produce less.

More suckling makes more milk.

Other effects of prolactin

Prolactin or other related hormones suppress the activity of the ovaries. So breastfeeding delays the return of fertility and menstruation (see Section 8.5).

Removal of milk

For milk production to continue, it is essential to *remove milk from the breast*. If milk is not removed, the breast secretes less. The pressure of the remaining milk on the gland cells decreases secretion.

The effect of removing milk is separate from the prolactin reflex. If a baby stops suckling from one breast, that breast stops producing milk—even if the baby continues to suckle the other breast and stimulates the prolactin reflex. So, removing milk helps milk production to continue. If the baby is not able to suckle for a time, the mother can remove milk by hand or with a pump (see Chapter 10).

2.4 OXYTOCIN—THE MILK EJECTING HORMONE

If you watch women breastfeeding, you sometimes see fine streams of milk flowing from the nipple. One stream comes from each duct. This is *milk ejection*. To eject means to throw out. Milk is ejected by small muscle cells around the breast glands which contract and increase the pressure on the milk inside. The pressure makes the milk flow along the ducts to the lactiferous sinuses and sometimes out through the nipple. The hormone *oxytocin* makes the muscle cells contract. Many women can feel the pressure in their breasts at the beginning of a feed. This tells them that their milk is starting to flow.

Oxytocin, like prolactin, is produced when the baby suckles and stimulates the sensory nerves in the nipple. Oxytocin is secreted by the posterior part of the pituitary gland and goes in the blood to the breasts.

9

Oxytocin works while the baby is suckling and makes the milk flow for *this* feed.

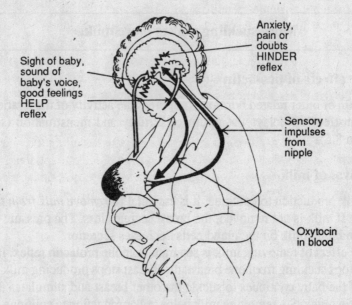

Figure 4. The oxytocin reflex or the milk ejection reflex.

These events are the milk ejection reflex, or the oxytocin reflex. A baby cannot get enough milk out of the breast just by suckling. He needs the ejection reflex to help him. If the reflex does not work then the baby may not get enough milk.

Helping and hindering the oxytocin reflex

The oxytocin reflex is more complicated than the prolactin reflex. The mother's thoughts, feelings and sensations can affect it. Usually her feelings help the reflex, but sometimes they hinder it.

Helping milk ejection

If a mother thinks lovingly of her baby, or if she hears him crying, her pituitary may produce oxytocin. Then she feels the pressure in her breasts and some milk may flow out. Her breasts are ready to feed her hungry baby.

10

Hindering milk ejection

Any of these feelings may hinder a woman's ejection reflex:
- If she is worried or afraid for some reason.
- If she is in pain—especially if breastfeeding is painful.
- If she is embarrassed.

So if a woman has good feelings, and is confident that she can breastfeed, her milk flows well. But if she doubts that she can breastfeed her baby, her worries may stop the milk from flowing.

Other effects of oxytocin

Oxytocin makes the uterus contract which helps to deliver the placenta. Breastfeeding may help to stop bleeding immediately after delivery and it shortens the time during which the mother loses lochia. A newly delivered mother may feel the contractions of the uterus when she breastfeeds. The pain can be quite strong and you need to reassure her that it is normal and that it will pass.

To help a mother's milk ejection:
Be kind and supportive.
Help her not to worry.
Reassure her that she can breastfeed.

2.5 HOW MILK IS PRODUCED

How milk "comes in"

For the first few days after delivery the breasts feel soft and empty. They secrete only small amounts of the yellowish first milk, called colostrum (see Section 3.4).

After a few days, the breasts begin to feel full and sometimes hard. They start to produce a lot of milk. We say that the milk has *"come in"*. Sometimes milk comes in in 2 days. Sometimes it takes nearly a week. It happens more quickly if the baby is allowed to feed whenever he wants to from the time of delivery. This is called *unrestricted* or *demand feeding* (see Sections 4.1 and 4.3).

Continuing milk production

After a few days the breasts feel less full. They become soft again though they continue to produce plenty of milk. Sometimes a mother thinks that her milk has dried up when her breasts become softer. You may need to reassure her that she has not lost her milk. If the baby continues to suckle whenever he is hungry, she will continue to make plenty of milk.

2.6 HOW BABIES SUCKLE

We call the special action of a baby at the breast *"suckling"*. *Sucking* is what a baby may do with his thumb, or any other solid object in his mouth.

The suckling reflexes

A healthy full-term baby has three reflexes which help him to feed.

The rooting reflex

This reflex helps a baby to find the nipple. If something touches the baby near his mouth, and he is hungry, he turns towards the touch and opens his mouth (see Figure 5).

The sucking reflex

When something goes into a baby's mouth far enough, and touches his palate, he sucks it. The sucking reflex may be very strong in the first hour after birth.

The swallowing reflex

If a baby's mouth fills with milk, he swallows it.

Notice that there is a reflex to help a baby to find the nipple, and a reflex to make him suck if the nipple touches his palate. But there is no reflex to help him take the breast into his mouth. That is something that he has to learn to do and for which he needs his mother's help.

The suckling action

It is helpful to think of suckling as two actions:

Stretching the breast tissue to form a teat

A baby does not take just the nipple into his mouth. He takes a mouthful of the areola and the breast tissue beneath which contains the lactiferous sinuses. The baby must pull out or stretch the breast tissue into a "teat" that is much longer than the "resting" nipple (see Figure 6b). The nipple forms only one-third of this "teat". You can sometimes see the long, stretched breast tissue for a moment when the baby stops suckling.

Pressing the stretched areola with the tongue against the palate

A wave (like peristalsis) goes along the tongue from the tip to the back near the baby's throat (see Figure 6c). The wave presses the milk out of the lactiferous sinuses into the baby's mouth so that he can swallow it. You can often see the tip of the baby's tongue over the lower lip while he suckles. The tongue is "cupping" the breast.

Notice two important points:

– Suction helps to pull out the breast tissue and hold it in the baby's mouth. Suction does not remove the milk.
– There should be no rubbing between the nipple skin and the baby's mouth.

Figure 5. The rooting reflex. When the nipple touches near the baby's mouth, he opens his mouth and tries to find the nipple.

13

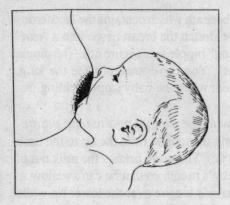

a. A baby suckling in a good position.

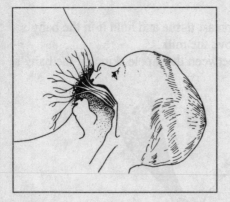

b. A good suckling position. The breast is stretched into a "teat" in the baby's mouth.

c. The wave going along the tongue to press the milk from the lactiferous sinuses.

Figure 6. How a baby suckles.

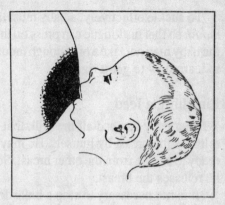

d. *A baby suckling in a poor position.*

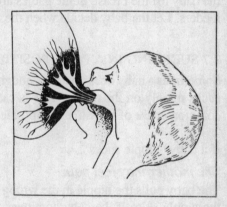

e. *A poor suckling position. The baby is sucking only the nipple and the tongue is held back in the mouth.*

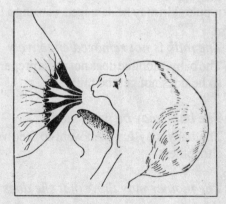

f. *A baby opening his mouth to take the breast. The nipple is aiming at his palate. His lower lip is aiming well below the nipple.*

Figure 6. How a baby suckles.

To suckle effectively, a baby must take *enough of the breast into his mouth* so that his tongue can press on the lactiferous sinuses. Sometimes the baby may not take a big enough mouthful. Both baby and mother have to learn how to get it right.

Finishing a feed

When a baby has had all the milk that he wants, he stops suckling and releases the breast by himself. He may have had enough, or he may be ready to suckle from the other breast. Sometimes the baby falls asleep as he releases the breast.

It is not necessary to stop a breastfeed after a certain time or to pull the baby off the breast. Some babies are slow feeders and some are fast feeders. Let the baby decide when the feed is finished.

2.7 SUCKLING IN A POOR POSITION

Sometimes a baby does not take enough of the breast into his mouth and sucks mainly on the nipple. This is called "nipple sucking" and it is a common cause of breastfeeding problems.

If a baby "nipple sucks":

The mother may feel pain

The baby pulls the nipple in the wrong way and his mouth rubs against the nipple skin. If the baby continues to suckle in a poor position the nipple skin may be damaged, causing a fissure (see Sections 5.3 and 5.4).

The milk is not removed effectively

The baby's tongue does not press properly against the lactiferous sinuses so he does not get the milk.

The baby may be frustrated

The baby may fuss and want to feed very often or may refuse to feed altogether.

The mother may think that she does not have enough milk

So a poor suckling position may be the cause of:
- Sore and cracked nipples.
- A poor milk supply and a baby who fails to grow.
- An unsatisfied baby who wants to feed all the time.
- A frustrated baby who refuses to feed.
- Engorged breasts.

There are several reasons for a poor suckling position.

The baby may have fed from a bottle
The baby may have had a few bottle feeds in the maternity ward while waiting for the breastmilk to "come in", or he may have had some bottle feeds later on.

The action of sucking from a feeding bottle is different. A rubber teat is already long enough and the baby does not have to stretch it out. A baby who has fed from a bottle may find it difficult afterwards to take the breast into his mouth. He may try to suck on his mother's nipple as if it were a rubber teat.

Difficulty feeding from a breast after using a bottle is sometimes called "nipple confusion".

The mother may be inexperienced
There may be no one who knows how to help her. She may have watched more babies bottle feeding than breastfeeding. She may offer her breast to the baby as if it were a bottle or she may "pinch" the nipple and try to push it into the baby's mouth.

The baby may be very small or weak
The baby may have difficulty taking enough of the breast into his mouth. Babies born preterm have difficulty co-ordinating their suckling movements.

There may be a problem with the nipple or breast
This may make it more difficult for the baby to take the breast.

If a baby is suckling in a poor position, mother and baby both need help to improve the position. The longer a baby suckles in a poor position the more difficult it can be to improve it.

2.8 HELPING A MOTHER TO PUT HER BABY ON TO THE BREAST

If you want to help a mother, you need to watch her baby feeding and decide if the position is good or poor (see Figures 6 and 7).

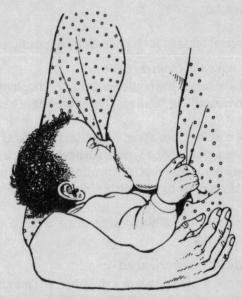

Figure 7. Baby suckling in a good position.

Signs that a baby is suckling in a good position

— The baby's whole body is facing his mother and is close to her.
— The baby's face is close up to the breast.
— The baby's chin is touching the breast.
— The baby's mouth is wide open.
— The baby's lower lip is curled outwards.
— There is more areola showing above the baby's upper lip and less areola showing below the lower lip.
— You can see the baby taking slow, deep sucks.
— The baby is relaxed and happy and is satisfied at the end of the feed.
— The mother does not feel nipple pain.
— You may be able to hear the baby swallowing.

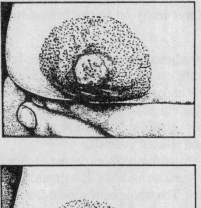

a. *Mother offering whole breast—this helps the baby to take enough of the breast into his mouth.*

b. *Mother offering nipple as if it were a rubber teat—this leads to the baby sucking only the nipple.*

Figure 8. Different ways to offer a breast to a baby.

Signs that the baby is suckling in a poor position

− The baby's body may be turned away from his mother's and not close to it.
− The baby's chin is separated from the breast (see Figure 10).
− The baby's mouth looks closed.
− The baby's lips point forwards.
− You see too much areola, including below the lower lip.
− The baby takes many quick, small sucks.
− The baby's cheeks may be pulled in as he sucks.
− The baby may fuss or refuse to feed because he does not get enough breastmilk.
− The mother may feel nipple pain.
− The baby's mouth may make a "smacking" sound as he sucks.
− The nipple may look flattened at the end of a feed and it may have a line across the tip.

How to help a mother put her baby on to the breast in a good position

- ❑ Let the mother sit or lie somewhere comfortable so that she is relaxed. A low seat is usually best. She can sit up and hold the baby in front, she can hold the baby's body under her arm, or she can lie down with the baby beside her. If it helps, she can support the baby on a cushion.
- ❑ Sit beside the mother so that you are at the same level as her and so that you are comfortable and relaxed yourself.
- ❑ Show her how to hold the baby so that he faces the breast. The baby's head should be in a straight line with his body. His stomach should be against the mother's stomach. The whole baby should face the breast and he should not have to turn or bend his head to suckle.
- ❑ If you need to hold the baby, hold him at the back of the shoulders — not the back of his head. His head should be free to bend back a little.
- ❑ The mother should lift her breast with her hand and offer the whole breast to the baby—not just the nipple (see Figure 8). She should not pinch the nipple or areola with her fingers or try to push the nipple into the baby's mouth.
- ❑ The mother can touch the baby's lips with the nipple to stimulate the rooting reflex. It is often best to touch the baby's upper lip.
- ❑ Wait until the baby's mouth is open wide and he wants to start feeding. Quickly move the baby well on to the breast.
- ❑ Aim the baby's lower lip well below the nipple. This helps to get the baby's chin close to the breast so that his tongue is right under the lactiferous sinuses. It helps to get the nipple above the centre of the baby's mouth so that it touches and stimulates the palate (see Figure 6f).

Some mothers like to put a finger on the breast near the baby's nose but this is not necessary and it may pull the breast out of the baby's mouth or make the suckling position worse. A baby can breathe quite well without the finger there.

Figure 9. A health worker helping a mother to put her baby on to the breast.

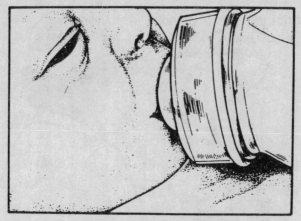

(a) A baby sucking from a bottle.

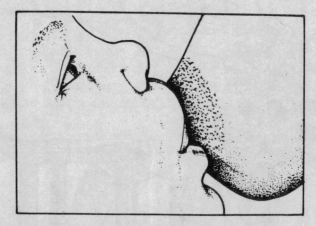

(b) A baby suckling from the breast in a poor position as if he were sucking from a bottle.

Figure 10. "Nipple sucking" is like sucking from a bottle.

2.9 SUCKLING FOR COMFORT

Babies suckle for closeness, comfort and pleasure as well as because they are hungry. Some babies need to suckle a lot. They suck on anything that goes into their mouths—their fingers, your finger, a dummy, a piece of cloth or plastic, and, of course, a nipple or teat. Many mothers think that a baby who wants to suck must be hungry. They give him a supplement which he does not need.

Comfort suckling from the breast

After the main feed from a breast the milk continues to flow, but more slowly. So if a baby continues to suckle he does not take too much milk.

Comfort sucking from a bottle

Milk from a bottle flows rapidly all the time. So if a baby continues to suck he may take too much milk and become unhealthy from overweight.

What to tell mothers about comfort suckling

- The baby needs to suckle for comfort as well as for food.
- The baby does *not* need a bottle or other supplement.
- If the baby cries he can suckle at the breast more.
- If the baby really is hungry or thirsty, suckling will increase the supply of milk.
- If the baby is restless and uncomfortable, the warmth, suckling and closeness will calm him down.

Babies suckle for comfort as well as from hunger.

CHAPTER THREE

The composition of breastmilk and the disadvantages of artificial feeding

Breastmilk is always in perfect condition for a baby, even if the woman is ill, pregnant, menstruating or undernourished.

3.1 WHY BREASTMILK IS A PERFECT FOOD

Breastmilk contains *all the nutrients* that a baby needs for the first 4–6 months and it is quickly and easily digested. It contains:
- The most suitable *protein* and *fat* for a baby, in the right quantities.
- More *lactose* (milk sugar) than most other milks, and that is what a human baby needs.
- Enough *vitamins* for the baby. Vitamin supplements are not necessary.
- Enough *iron* for the baby. There is not a large amount of iron but it is well absorbed from the baby's intestine. Breastfed babies do not develop iron deficiency anaemia.
- Enough *water* for the baby, even in a hot, dry climate.
- The correct amounts of *salt*, *calcium* and *phosphate*.
- A special *enzyme* (lipase) which digests fat.

3.2 HOW BREASTMILK PROTECTS BABIES AGAINST INFECTION

Breastmilk is clean and free of bacteria so it cannot make a baby ill. It contains *anti-infective* factors which prevent infection. These include:
- Living *white blood cells* (leucocytes) which kill bacteria.
- *Antibodies* (immunoglobulins) to many common infections which protect a baby until he can make his own antibodies. If a mother has

an infection, antibodies against that infection soon appear in her milk.
- A substance called the *bifidus factor* which helps special bacteria called *Lactobacillus bifidus* to grow in the baby's intestine. *Lactobacillus bifidus* prevents other harmful bacteria from growing and causing diarrhoea.
- *Lactoferrin* which binds iron. This prevents the growth of some harmful bacteria which need iron.

Breastfed babies have less diarrhoea and fewer respiratory and middle-ear infections than artificially fed babies. A baby who continues to breastfeed during an infection recovers more quickly than a baby who stops breastfeeding. It is not necessary to stop breastmilk feeds if a baby has diarrhoea.

Breastmilk continues to help prevent illness and to help children recover during the second and third years of life.

Babies who are breastfed have fewer infections.

3.3 THE OTHER ADVANTAGES OF BREASTFEEDING

Bonding

Breastfeeding helps a mother and baby to develop a close, loving bond (see Section 4.1). Having a close relationship with his mother may help a child to form good relationships with other people. It helps the child to develop normally.

If a mother bottle feeds her baby, it is easier to give the baby to someone else to feed, or to leave the bottle beside the baby so that he has to feed himself. The baby may get less affection and stimulation.

The mother's health

Breastfeeding helps to stop bleeding after delivery and it helps the mother to regain her normal figure. Frequent breastfeeding helps to protect against another pregnancy (see Section 8.5).

Convenience

- Breastmilk is always ready to give to the baby and it needs no preparation.
- Breastmilk never goes sour or bad in the breast even if a woman does not feed her baby for some days. Some mothers believe that breastmilk can go sour in the breast. You may need to reassure them that it does not.
- Breastmilk is cheap—you do not have to buy it.
- Breastmilk is all for the baby. It does not have to be shared among the family or visitors. Other milks may be used for someone's tea.

3.4 CHANGES IN THE COMPOSITION OF BREASTMILK

Breastmilk does not always have exactly the same composition. There are some important normal variations. Breastmilk also varies slightly with the woman's diet, but these changes seldom matter.

Occasionally, a mother finds that some unusual food that she eats upsets her baby (see Section 6.4), but most mothers can continue to eat their normal food while they breastfeed. Even strong spices, such as chilli pepper, do not usually affect the milk or upset the baby.

Colostrum

For the first few days after delivery, the breasts secrete *colostrum*. Colostrum is yellow and thicker than later milk, and it is secreted in only small amounts. But it is enough for a normal baby and it is exactly what a baby needs for the first few days.

Colostrum contains more antibodies and more white blood cells than later milk. It gives a baby his first "immunization" to protect him against most of the bacteria and viruses that he will meet.

Colostrum is also rich in growth factors which stimulate a baby's immature intestine to develop. The growth factors prepare the baby's intestine to digest and absorb milk, and to prevent the absorption of undigested protein. If a baby has cow's milk or other foods before having colostrum, the foods can damage the intestine and cause allergies.

Colostrum is laxative and helps the baby to pass meconium (the first, very dark stools). This helps to prevent jaundice.

In some communities it is the custom not to let the baby have colostrum. Health workers should discuss the protective value of colostrum with people in these communities and encourage them to change this practice.

Colostrum is exactly what a baby needs for the first few days.

Mature milk

During the next 1–2 weeks, the milk increases in quantity and changes in appearance and composition. This is the *mature milk*. Mature breastmilk looks thinner than cow's milk which makes some mothers think that their milk is too thin. But it contains all the nutrients that a baby needs to grow. You may need to reassure mothers that this watery appearance is normal. It may help to explain that a baby gets all the water that he needs from breastmilk, even in very hot weather.

Foremilk and hindmilk

The composition of breastmilk changes during a feed.

Foremilk comes at the beginning of a feed. It looks grey and watery. It is rich in protein, lactose, vitamins, minerals and water.

Hindmilk comes at the end of a feed. It looks whiter than foremilk because it contains more fat. The fat makes the hindmilk rich in energy. Fat supplies more than half the energy in breastmilk.

A baby needs both the foremilk and the hindmilk for growth and development. It is important not to take a slow feeder off the breast before he has finished or he may not get enough hindmilk.

3.5 BREASTFEEDING AND BOWEL MOVEMENTS

The number of stools that a breastfed baby passes is very variable, especially in the early weeks.

A breastfed baby may not pass a stool for several days. This is *not* constipation. It is a sign that breastmilk is a perfect food. It is almost all absorbed into the baby's body and there is very little waste.

A breastfed baby may pass eight or more very soft stools a day. But this is *not* diarrhoea. It is important to know the difference between the soft stools of a breastfed infant and the watery stools of diarrhoea.

It is very uncommon for a breastfed baby to have hard stools. Many babies appear to "strain" as they pass a stool, but this is normal. It does not mean that the stool is difficult to pass. Apparent discomfort may be commoner if the baby passes stools infrequently. True constipation with hard stools is more common in artificially fed babies.

3.6 THE DISADVANTAGES OF ARTIFICIAL FEEDING

Contamination

Artificial feeds are often contaminated with bacteria, especially if the mother uses a feeding bottle. They can be dangerous to a baby long before the milk smells sour. Bottles are difficult to clean and need to be boiled after every feed. Bacteria grow in artificial feeds very quickly, especially in a feeding bottle which is left around in the warm.

Infections

Artificial feeds do not contain anti-infective factors. Artificially fed babies are ill more often with diarrhoea and other infections—even if the feeds are cleanly prepared.

Persistent diarrhoea

In artificially fed babies, diarrhoea is more likely to become persistent— that is, to continue for more than 2 weeks. Persistent diarrhoea can be difficult to treat and may lead to severe undernutrition. It is sometimes necessary to stop giving the baby artificial milk feeds to cure the condition.

Artificially fed babies are ill more often.

Lack of vitamins

Cow's milk may not contain enough vitamins for a baby, especially vitamin C. So artificially fed babies may need fruit juice.

Lack of iron

The iron from cow's milk is not absorbed as completely as the iron from breastmilk. An artificially fed baby may develop iron deficiency anaemia. Manufacturers often add iron to infant formula to prevent iron deficiency but added iron may increase the risk of infection in the baby.

Bottle feeding causes malnutrition.

Too much salt

Cow's milk contains too much salt which can sometimes cause hypernatraemia (too much salt in the blood) and fits, especially if the child has diarrhoea.

Too much calcium and phosphate

This may cause tetany, that is, twitching and spasms of muscles.

Unsuitable fat

Cow's milk contains more saturated fatty acids than breastmilk. For healthy growth, a baby needs more unsaturated fatty acids.

Cow's milk does not contain enough of the essential fatty acid called linoleic acid, and it may not contain enough cholesterol for the growing brain.

Dried skimmed milk (DSM) contains no fat so it does not contain enough energy.

Unsuitable protein

Cow's milk contains too much of the protein casein. Casein contains an unsuitable mixture of amino acids which are difficult for a baby's immature kidneys to excrete.

Health workers sometimes teach mothers to dilute cow's milk with water to reduce the total protein. However, the diluted milk may not contain enough of the essential amino acids *cystine* and *taurine* which are needed for the baby's growing brain. Manufacturers sometimes add taurine to formula.

Indigestion

Cow's milk is more difficult to digest. It does not contain the enzyme lipase to digest the fat. Also, the casein forms thick, indigestible curds. Because cow's milk is digested slowly, it fills the stomach for longer than breastmilk, so the baby does not become hungry again as quickly as he should. The baby's stools become thicker and harder and he may become constipated.

Allergy

Babies who are fed on cow's milk early are more likely to have allergic problems, for example asthma and eczema, and cow's milk intolerance.

Suckling problems

A baby who learns to suck from a bottle may have difficulty suckling from the breast and may refuse altogether. A few bottle feeds can cause breastfeeding failure.

Expense

Poor mothers may be unable to buy enough milk for their babies. They may give too few feeds and they may put too little milk or milk powder into each bottle. They may make dilute feeds of cereal instead. Bottle fed babies often become severely malnourished.

3.7 EXCLUSIVE AND PARTIAL BREASTFEEDING

Exclusive breastfeeding means that the baby has no other food or drink but breastmilk—not even a "dummy" (or "pacifier"). If the baby has vitamins, or small amounts of ritual food, or a few sips of water or juice, he is *almost exclusively* breastfed.

Partial breastfeeding means that the baby breastfeeds part of the time but has some artificial feeds or supplements.

The best and safest way to feed a baby is exclusive breastfeeding. Babies do not normally need anything else, even in the first few days after they are born, until they are 4–6 months old. If they are given other food or drinks, even in small amounts, or if they suck on a dummy, some of the advantages of breastfeeding may be lost. Babies can get diarrhoea or allergies, and mothers are more likely to conceive again.

However, partial breastfeeding is better than not breastfeeding at all.

3.8 THE COST OF ARTIFICIAL FEEDS

(Prices from Kenya mid-1990. At that time $US1 = KSh 25.)
Health educators and counsellors should point out to mothers:
- The cost of feeding a baby with *enough* milk.
- The danger of giving the baby less milk to try to save money.
- The importance of following the instructions on the label if they use formula.

Encourage mothers to think of the difficulty and expense of *several months* of artificial feeding. If a mother buys only one or two tins every now and then, the baby will not grow well. Some fathers bring their wives a tin of formula after the delivery. They think that they are making a kind gesture. Will they continue to give her money every month to buy more baby milk?

If the woman has to work to support the family herself, she also needs to think of the cost. How much can she save if she feeds the baby as much as possible on breastmilk?

Cost of feeding a baby fresh cow's milk for 6 months

How much milk does a baby need?

On average, a baby needs 150 ml milk per kilo of his body weight each day.

So a 3.5 kg baby needs 525 ml per day, a 5 kg baby needs 750 ml per day, and a 7 kg baby needs about 1 litre a day.

If a baby follows a normal growth curve in the first 6 months, he will need a total of 135 litres of fresh milk.

How much does the milk cost?

Half-litre KCC tetrapaks of milk cost KSh 3.90 each. So the cost will be KSh 1,053 for 6 months (average KSh 170.50 per month).

If the mother buys milk from a neighbour, she may have to pay KSh

3 for half a litre, so the cost would be KSh 810 for 6 months (average KSh 135 per month).

Cost of feeding a baby on powdered full-cream milk for 6 months

How much milk powder does a baby need?
On average, a baby needs about 2 kg of powdered milk each month for the first 3 months, and about 2.5 kg each month after that age. This makes a total of 13.5 kg, or 27 half-kilo tins, for 6 months.

How much does the milk powder cost?
One half-kilo tin of Safariland costs KSh 52.20. The cost would be KSh 1,409.40 for 6 months (average KSh 234.90 per month).

Cost of feeding a baby on locally manufactured formula feeds for 6 months

How much formula does a baby need?
In the first month of life he needs 5 half-kilo tins of Nan, in his second month, 6.5 tins and in his third month, 8 tins. If the mother then changes to Lactogen, she needs 8 tins each month for the next 3 months, which is a total of 24 tins.

How much does the formula cost?
One tin of Nan costs KSh 67.80, so the cost of 19.5 tins for the first 3 months is KSh 1,322.10.

One tin of Lactogen costs KSh 46.90, so the cost of 24 tins is KSh 1,126.60.

So the total cost of formula is KSh 2,448.70 for 6 months (average KSh 408.10 per month).

Minimum wage

The minimum wage for an urban general labourer in Kenya in 1990 is KSh 723 per month. In rural areas, the unskilled wage is KSh 448 per month. For those under the age of 18 years, the wage is KSh 320 per month.

Many women, particularly those in domestic service, earn less than the minimum wage.

Conclusions

Any artificial feeding takes a large part of a family's income, which other family members need for food and other expenses, such as school fees and school uniforms.

In town, the cheapest artificial feed is KCC milk bought in tetrapaks. To feed an infant fully on this milk costs almost one quarter of the minimum wage. The more expensive formulas cost more than half of the urban minimum wage.

In rural areas, a woman may be able to buy milk more cheaply from a neighbour. If so, she may be able to feed a baby artificially for one-sixth of the minimum government salary. But if the family is living on an agricultural wage, cow's milk uses nearly one-third of their income. To feed a baby on formula takes almost all of an agricultural worker's income—91%.

For a single mother under the age of 18 years, it costs nearly half her salary to buy cow's milk. She cannot afford formula at all.

Artificial feeds can cost most of a family's income.

Note: Formula is similar to cow's milk. The more expensive brands are "modified" so that they are more like human milk. They contain less salt, less protein, less calcium and more sugar than cow's milk, ordinary tinned milk, or cheaper brands of formula. However, the quality of protein and fat can never equal that of breastmilk, and no formula can contain anti-infective substances. Also, if formula is mixed incorrectly, it can contain too much salt, etc.

Dried skimmed milk (DSM) has all the disadvantages of formula *and* it lacks fat, so it does not contain enough energy for a baby.

Table 1. Comparison of Human Milk and Cow's Milk

	Human	Cow's
Bacterial contamination	None	Likely
Anti-infective substances	Antibodies Leucocytes	Not active
	Lactoferrin Bifidus factor	Not present
Protein		
Total	1%	4% too much
Casein	0.5%	3% too much
Lactalbumen	0.5%	0.5%
Amino-acids		
Cystine	Enough for growing brain	Not enough
Taurine		
Fat		
Total	4% (average)	4%
Saturation of fatty acids	Enough unsaturated	Too much saturated
Linoleic acid (essential)	Enough for growing brain	Not enough
Cholesterol	Enough	Not enough
Lipase to digest fat	Present	None
Lactose (sugar)	7% — enough	3–4% — not enough
Salts (mEq/l)		
Sodium	6.5 correct amount	25 too much
Chloride	12 correct amount	29 too much
Potassium	14 correct amount	35 too much
Minerals (mg/l)		
Calcium	350 correct amount	1,400 too much
Phosphate	150 correct amount	900 too much
Iron	Small amount Well absorbed Enough	Small amount Poorly absorbed Not enough
Vitamins	Enough	May not be enough
Water	Enough No extra needed	Extra needed

CHAPTER FOUR

How breastfeeding should begin

The first few days after delivery are very important. Mothers are more likely to succeed and to continue with breastfeeding if the baby stays with them from the time of birth, and if they get skilled help and support from the beginning.

Most of the recommendations in this chapter are reinforced by the Directive from the Kenya Director of Medical Services sent to all hospitals in June 1983.*

The baby should start to feed soon after birth.

4.1 THE FIRST FEED

❏ As soon as the baby is born, let the mother hold him close. If it is acceptable, the baby should be naked and the mother can hold him against her naked chest so that they have skin-to-skin contact. Dry the baby and cover them both to keep them warm.

❏ Encourage the mother to let the baby suckle. There is no need to force the baby to suckle immediately but most babies are ready to try within about an hour. They may be very alert at this time and their suckling reflex may be strong.

---

* Ministry of Health Reference MIS/17/4/106 Vol. VII(114) 1, 15 June 1983.

This early contact in the first hour or so is important for bonding (see Section 3.3). It helps a mother to love and care for her baby and she is more likely to breastfeed for a long time. If mother and baby are separated for even a few hours, breastfeeding is more likely to fail. The mother may be more likely to abandon her baby.

Suckling stimulates the production of oxytocin which may help to deliver the placenta and stop haemorrhage.

The baby gets valuable colostrum. Starting early makes it easier for the baby to learn to suckle in a good position.

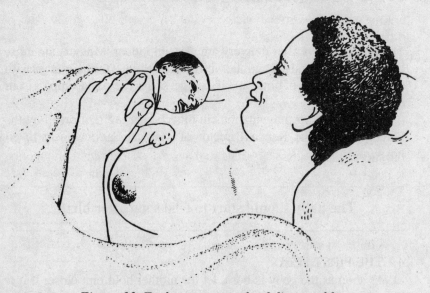

Figure 11. Early contact on the delivery table.

4.2 KEEPING MOTHER AND BABY TOGETHER

There is no need for a mother and baby to rest separately after a normal delivery. She should have the baby with her, in her bed or in a small cot beside her bed. This is called *rooming-in* or *bedding-in*. The mother can respond to the baby from the beginning. She can breastfeed him and clean him whenever it is necessary and hold him when she wants to.

It is quite safe for a baby to sleep in the same bed as his mother. She will not lie on him unless she is very ill, sedated, or drunk. We now know that "cot death" (sudden infant death syndrome) is more likely when the baby sleeps apart from the mother and it is not due to the mother lying on the baby.

Rooming-in helps to prevent many breastfeeding problems and there is less work for the ward staff.

The baby should stay in or near the mother's bed.

4.3 UNRESTRICTED BREASTFEEDING

Let the mother breastfeed whenever the baby seems to want to. This is often called *demand feeding*.

Babies may feed very irregularly at first: they may feed only a few times in the first day or two; then they may feed very often for several days. Every baby is different, but most settle down into some sort of rhythm after a week or two. Making a baby feed only at special times interferes with breastfeeding.

Frequent, unrestricted suckling from soon after birth stimulates the production of prolactin which helps the breastmilk to "come in" sooner. It helps to prevent engorgement and the problems which follow (see Section 5.1).

The baby should feed whenever he wants to from birth.

Problems with unrestricted feeding

The baby does not demand often enough
Some babies are too quiet and they do not cry when they are hungry. Think of this if a baby does not gain weight fast enough (see Section 6.3).
❑ Discuss with the mother how she can feed the baby *more often* than he demands.

The baby demands to be fed too often
Some babies seem to want to feed continuously and they exhaust their mothers.

- Sometimes this is because they are suckling in a poor position so they are not getting enough milk (see Section 2.7).
- Sometimes it is because they feed for too short a time at each breast.

❏ Help the mother to improve her breastfeeding technique. (See also Section 6.5 on Crying.)

Figure 12. Let a mother have her baby in bed with her.

4.4 LENGTH OF BREASTFEEDS

Formerly, health workers advised mothers to give very short feeds, for example, 2–3 minutes for the first few days and 5–10 minutes later on. They believed that suckling for too long caused sore nipples.

Now we know that the length of a breastfeed does not matter. It is suckling in a poor position that causes sore nipples (see Section 5.3).

❏ Make sure that the baby is suckling in a good position.
❏ Then let him suckle as long as he wants to.

Babies vary in how long they take to breastfeed. Most finish in 5–10 minutes, but some take 20–30 minutes. It does not matter.

New research has shown that slow feeders take the same total amount of milk as fast feeders. If you stop a slow feeder before he is ready, he may not take enough milk. He may not get the energy-rich hindmilk that he needs to grow well (see Section 3.5).

Let the baby feed when he wants and for as long as he wants.

4.5 FEEDING FROM BOTH BREASTS

Larger babies may want both breasts at every feed. Smaller babies may be satisfied after one breast only, or they may take only a little milk from the second breast.

Many mothers have a "favourite" side. However, if the baby suckles more from one side than the other, the "neglected" breast may become engorged, or may stop making milk. The favourite breast may become larger. Babies can often get enough milk from one breast only, so it may not matter, but usually it is better to use both breasts equally.

Some mothers take the baby off the first breast before he has finished to make sure that he takes the second breast. Then the baby may get too much foremilk and not enough hindmilk, which can cause problems (see Section 6.4).

Encourage mothers to:
- ❏ Let the baby finish the first breast to make sure that he gets the hindmilk. Offer the second breast and let him take it if he wants to, but do not force him.
- ❏ Start feeding from the right breast at one feed and from the left breast at the next feed. Then both breasts have the same amount of stimulation and both continue to produce milk.
- ❏ If the baby does not want to take one side, the mother can try to hold him in a different position—for example, under her arm (as for twins, see Figure 28). This may make the other breast seem more like the favourite breast to the baby.

Let the baby finish the first breast before you offer the second.

4.6 PRELACTEAL FEEDS

It has been the practice in many hospitals to give babies *prelacteal* feeds. These are feeds of formula, cow's milk, or glucose water, given before the mother's milk "comes in". Health workers sometimes fear that the baby might be hungry or might become dehydrated in the first few days before the mother has breastmilk in large quantities.

We now know that prelacteal feeds are not necessary. They can make the baby ill and they can interfere with breastfeeding. Colostrum is all that a normal baby needs at this time. Many experts now believe that you can safely give breastmilk for a baby's first "test feed".

Dangers of prelacteal feeds

For the baby
- He may not want to suckle from the breast because the artificial feeds stop him feeling hungry or thirsty.
- He does not get colostrum.
- Diarrhoea and other infections are more likely, especially if the artificial feed is contaminated.
- Allergic conditions are more likely if the baby has cow's milk very early.
- The baby may get nipple confusion if he takes the feeds from a bottle (see Section 2.7).

For the mother
- Breastmilk takes longer to come in because the baby does not suckle enough.
- Engorgement (see Section 5.1) and mastitis (see Section 5.8) are more likely because the baby does not remove the milk.
- The mother has more difficulty establishing breastfeeding and is more likely to stop.
  Even two prelacteal feeds may cause breastfeeding failure.

4.7 EXTRA WATER

A normal baby is born with a store of water which keeps him well hydrated until the milk comes in. He does not need drinks of water or glucose water: they interfere with breastfeeding (see Section 9.3).

A baby does not need extra water—even in hot weather.

4.8 NIGHT BREASTFEEDS

Some mothers try to make their babies sleep all through the night, without feeding. It is better if the mother breastfeeds the baby at night as long as he wants to. The easiest way is to let the baby sleep with her so that he can breastfeed without disturbing her.

Breastfeeding at night gives the baby extra time for suckling. More prolactin is secreted at night than during the day. This:
- Helps to keep up the milk supply.
- Helps if the mother is away for part of the day, for example at work. The baby gets much of the milk that he needs at night and he needs less milk during the day.
- Is important for child spacing (see Section 8.5).

The baby should breastfeed at night for as long as possible.

4.9 EARLY WEIGHT CHANGES

A baby may lose weight for the first few days after delivery. He may lose up to 10% of his birth weight.

When the milk comes in, the baby begins to gain weight. He should return to his birth weight within about 10 days.

Babies who demand feed from birth lose less weight than babies who feed only at certain times, and they regain their birth weight sooner.

A baby should regain his birth weight in 10 days.

4.10 CLEANING THE BREASTS

In the past, health workers in hospitals have taught mothers to wash their nipples before every feed. We now know that this is not necessary and it can damage the nipple skin.

Frequent washing, especially with soap, removes the natural oil from the skin of the nipple and areola (see Section 2.1). The skin becomes dry and is more easily damaged and fissured (cracked). In any case, most women do not have time to wash before every feed—especially if they demand feed.

Do not wash nipples with soap—it can damage the skin.

CHAPTER FIVE

Early problems

The first few weeks of breastfeeding can be a difficult time, especially for a mother having her first baby. You can prevent many problems if you give mothers the support that they need in the first few days.

5.1 "MY BREASTS ARE TOO FULL AND THEY HURT"

When the milk first comes in, the breasts may feel hot, heavy and hard. They may feel as though they are full of stones. This fullness is due partly to the milk that now fills the breast and partly to an increase in the amount of blood and fluid in the supporting tissue.

In most cases, the breasts are simply full. The milk continues to flow and the baby can feed normally. The mother should feed the baby frequently to remove the milk. If feeding does not relieve the fullness, she can express some milk. After some days the breasts will feel less full. However, she will continue to produce plenty of milk.

Sometimes, especially if not enough milk is removed, the breasts may become *engorged*. Engorged breasts are painful. They look tight and shiny because of oedema (fluid) in the tissues. The milk may stop flowing.

Engorgement is commoner after hospital delivery than after home delivery. It is commonest in hospitals where babies are given prelacteal feeds, where they are only allowed to feed at certain times, or where there are long intervals between feeds (for example at night).

Engorgement is less common where babies stay with their mothers day and night, and where they breastfeed from soon after birth, exclusively and without any restrictions.

After some days engorgement usually stops. However, you must help the woman to keep comfortable and to continue breastfeeding the baby. If you do not help her, breastfeeding may fail.

How engorgement leads to breastfeeding failure

- The areola is tight and it is difficult for the baby to stretch the breast out to form a teat.
- The baby suckles in a poor position and does not remove the milk effectively.
- Suckling in a poor position damages the nipple skin and may cause a fissure.
- The mother feeds the baby less because it hurts her.
- The milk supply decreases because the baby does not suckle often enough and the milk is not removed.
- The breast may become infected (mastitis, breast abscess, see Section 5.2). Infection may enter through a nipple fissure.

To prevent engorgement, take the milk from the breasts
- ❏ Let mothers breastfeed their babies without restrictions from soon after delivery.
- ❏ Make sure that the baby suckles in a good position from the first day.
- ❏ Do not give any prelacteal feeds.

To treat engorgement, take the milk from the breasts
- ❏ The baby should continue to breastfeed if possible.
- ❏ If the baby cannot suckle effectively, help the mother to express the milk. She may be able to express by hand (see Section 10.1). If the breasts are too painful, she can use a pump (see Section 10.2), or try the "warm bottle" technique (see Section 10.3).
- ❏ After she has expressed some of the milk, the breasts should be softer. Then it may be possible for the baby to take enough breast into his mouth to suckle more effectively.
- ❏ If the baby cannot suckle at all, give him the expressed breastmilk (EBM) by cup.
- ❏ Continue to express as often as necessary to make the breasts comfortable until the engorgement stops.

Milk fever

Sometimes a woman with engorged breasts has a fever for 24 hours. This is called "milk fever" and it is probably caused by substances from the milk passing into the woman's blood. Usually the fever stops without treatment. If it continues for more than 48 hours, look for infection (see Section 5.2).

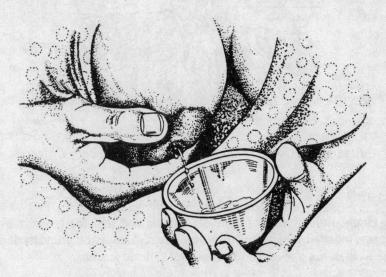

Figure 13. Expressing milk to treat engorgement.

5.2 "THERE IS A PAINFUL SWELLING IN MY BREAST"

Blocked duct

The gland tissue in the breast is arranged in 10–20 sections or segments like a lemon (see Figure 14). A duct leads from each segment. Sometimes the milk from one segment of the breast does not drain, possibly because thickened milk blocks the duct from that segment.

A painful lump forms in the breast. In light-skinned women, the skin over the lump may look red. The woman feels well and has no fever. The exact cause is not clear, but it may be the result of tight clothing, or the baby not suckling that part of the breast efficiently.

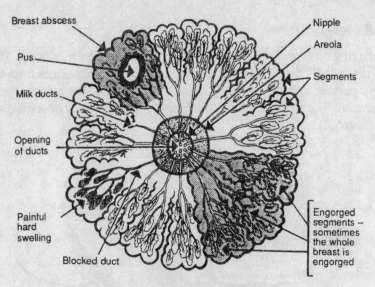

Figure 14. How the breast is arranged in segments. Different kinds of swelling.

Mastitis

If a blocked duct or engorged breast is not cleared, the breast tissue may become infected. Part of the breast becomes red, hot, swollen and tender. The woman has a fever and feels unwell. This is *mastitis*.

Unrestricted breastfeeding helps to prevent mastitis.

Breast abscess

If mastitis is not treated early, it may develop into an *abscess*.

There is a painful, hot swelling which becomes fluctuant—that is, it feels as though it is full of fluid.

Breast abscess can also occur without mastitis—the breast is softer and the woman is not so ill. This may happen later on when the child is older.

To treat a blocked duct

Treat a blocked duct carefully to prevent mastitis and breast abscess. Usually it clears in a day or two.

❏ Help the mother to improve the suckling position.

❏ Show her different positions for feeding the baby to make sure that milk is removed from all segments of the breast. She can sit up instead of lying down. She can hold the baby under her arm, instead of across the front.

❏ Encourage her to feed the baby frequently from the breast with the swelling.

❏ Show her how to gently massage the lump towards the nipple to help to empty that part of the breast.

❏ Encourage her to take some rest and to wear loose clothes.

To treat mastitis or breast abscess

To treat an infected breast, you must remove the milk. Antibiotics and other treatments do not help if the milk remains in the breast. It is not necessary to "rest" the breast, but it is important for the woman herself to rest.

❏ The mother should take sick leave from her employment and rest as much as possible. If she continues to work, the infection may recur.

❏ Encourage her to continue to feed the baby from the breast. It is safe to do so and it will not make the baby ill. Probably the bacteria that are growing in the breast are also growing in the baby.

❏ If the mother does not want the baby to suckle from the infected breast she *must* express the milk. If the milk stays in the breast, the infection may spread and her milk may dry up completely.
  – Show her how to express by hand or with a pump.
  – Explain that she must express several times a day.
  – Help her to continue to feed the baby on the other breast.

❏ Give a suitable course of antibiotics.

❏ Give aspirin tablets for the pain and fever.

❏ Show her how to put a cloth soaked in warm water on the breast to relieve the pain. She should do this several times a day.

❏ If an abscess forms, refer her to hospital for incision and drainage.

❏ Help her to start breastfeeding again from the infected breast as soon as possible. She should let the baby suckle again after one or two days.

❑ Follow her up after treatment to make sure that she continues to breastfeed. Help her to build up her milk supply again (see Section 10.5).

A woman with mastitis must take time off work.
Rest the mother, not the breast.

5.3 "MY NIPPLES ARE SORE"

The commonest cause of sore nipples is the baby *suckling in a poor position*. He does not have enough of the breast in his mouth, and he sucks only the nipple.

The nipple skin may look completely normal. But if you watch the baby finishing a feed, you may notice the nipple looks flattened as it comes out of the baby's mouth. There may be a line across the tip of the nipple.

How sore nipples can cause breastfeeding failure
– Feeding is painful so the mother feeds the baby less often and for a shorter time.
– When the baby sucks only the nipple, he does not get much milk.
– The milk is not removed from the breasts so the supply decreases.

To prevent sore nipples
❑ Help mothers to get their babies to suckle in a good position from the first day.
❑ Ask mothers in your care if breastfeeding is comfortable. Sometimes new mothers do not know what breastfeeding should feel like, or they expect to feel pain. They may think that the pain they feel is "normal". A woman may feel a very brief pain at the beginning of the first few feeds. If she has more pain than this, there is a problem. If she is doubtful, or if she looks uncomfortable, help her to improve the suckling position anyway.
❑ Advise mothers not to wash their nipples more than once a day and not to use soap.

❑ To take the baby off the breast at the end of a feed:
  – Wait until the baby releases the breast.
  – If the mother has to take the baby off the breast for some reason, she should put her finger gently into the baby's mouth to break the suction first.
  It is *not* necessary to limit the duration of feeds (see Section 4.4).

A poor suckling position is the commonest cause of sore nipples.

To treat sore nipples

❑ Try to find and treat sore nipples before the skin is damaged.
❑ Help the mother to improve the baby's suckling position. In most cases the pain stops immediately. You may see the mother's face suddenly change when the baby takes enough of the breast into his mouth. She may exclaim that it feels different and "right" and that it is now comfortable and pleasurable. The baby may be more satisfied at the end of a feed.
❑ It is not usually necessary to stop the baby feeding from the breast, even for a few feeds.
❑ It is not necessary to put creams or other medicines on to the nipples. They do not help and they may make the soreness worse.

If the soreness continues for more than a week, or if it starts after a period of pain-free breastfeeding, it may be due to thrush (candida infection). Sometimes thrush from the baby's mouth spreads to the mother's nipples. The pain may be itchy; or there may be a sharp pain which seems to go deep into the breast.

❑ Look at the nipples—you may see white spots.
❑ Check the baby's mouth for the white spots of thrush.
❑ Put nystatin cream or gentian violet on the nipples and put nystatin drops or gentian violet in the baby's mouth.
❑ If there is deep pain, give the mother nystatin tablets (500,000 units 4 times a day for 10 days) or miconazole tablets (250 mg 4 times a day for 10 days) to take by mouth.

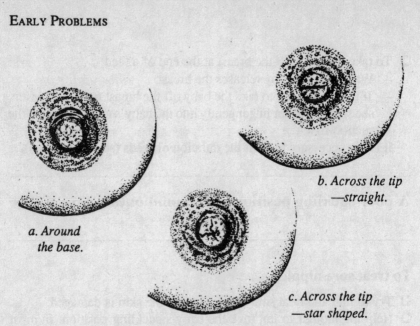

*b. Across the tip
—straight.*

*a. Around
the base.*

*c. Across the tip
—star shaped.*

Figure 15. Different shapes of nipple fissure.

5.4 "MY NIPPLES ARE CRACKED"

If a baby continues to feed in a poor position, it may damage the nipple skin. Then a *fissure*, or crack, appears.

If the nipple skin is damaged, bacteria can enter the breast tissue and cause mastitis or breast abscess more easily. Infection is most likely if the baby has stopped feeding from the breast so that the milk is not removed.

To treat a fissure

❑ Advise the mother to stop using any soaps, sprays or medicated creams on the nipple. They can make the soreness worse. Advise her to wash her nipples only once a day when she washes her body in the ordinary way.

❑ Help the mother to improve the suckling position and continue to breastfeed the baby. She can start breastfeeds on the side that is not sore. Often the pain improves immediately and the fissure heals very quickly when the position improves.

❑ She can expose the nipples to the air and sun as much as possible between breastfeeds.

❑ She can leave a drop of hindmilk on the nipple after each breastfeed—it helps the skin to heal.

If the mother cannot continue to feed the baby from the breast

Sometimes the pain continues after you improve the feeding position. Sometimes the breast is engorged and the baby cannot take enough of the breast into his mouth. Then you must *remove the milk another way* while the fissure heals.

❑ Show the mother how to express her milk. Let her feed the EBM to the baby by cup for a few feeds (see Sections 10.1 and 10.2).

5.5 "MY NIPPLES ARE FLAT"

Some women think that their nipples are too short for breastfeeding. However, the *length* of the "resting" nipple is not important. The baby suckles the breast and not the nipple. Think of the nipple as a "marker" to show the baby where to take the breast. What is important is for the areola and breast tissue beneath to pull out or *protract* to form the "teat" (see Section 2.6).

There are many nipples which look flat or short, but the breast tissue protracts well and causes no problem.

Other nipples seem not to protract well, but they develop and improve during pregnancy. They improve more after delivery when the baby suckles and stretches them.

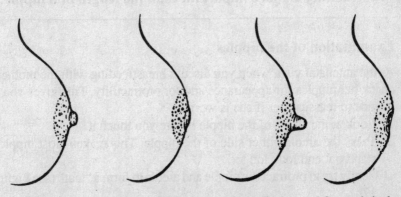

a. *Average nipple.*   b. *Short or flat nipple.*   c. *Long nipple.*   d. *Inverted nipple.*

Figure 16. Different nipple shapes.

Occasionally a nipple really does not protract well. If you try to pull it out, it goes deeper into the breast. This is an *inverted nipple*.

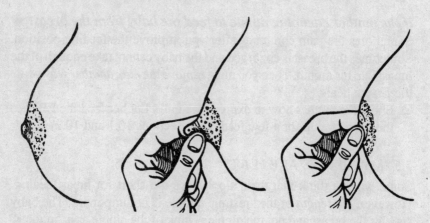

a. A short nipple. Is it protractile or not?

b. If you can pull it out like this, then it protracts well.

c. If it goes in like this when you try to pull it out, then it is not protractile.

Figure 17. Testing a nipple for protractility.

Protractility is more important than the length of a nipple.

Examination of the nipples

At the antenatal visit, when you discuss breastfeeding with the mother, check her nipples for appearance and for protractility. This gives you a chance to reassure her if she is worried.

- ❑ Look at the shape of the nipple before you touch it.
- ❑ Press the areola either side of the nipple. This makes most nipples stand out and look longer.
- ❑ Gently try to protract the nipple and areola to form a "teat" (see Figure 17b).
  - If the nipple pulls out easily, it is protractile.

- If the nipple pulls out very little, it is poorly protractile.
- If the nipple does not pull out but goes in deeper, then it is inverted.

How to help a woman with flat nipples

If her nipples protract easily:
❏ Reassure her that she has good nipples, even if they look flat.

If one or both nipples do not protract well:
❏ Reassure the woman that she can breastfeed.
❏ Explain how the baby suckles from the breast, not the nipple. Explain that the baby can feed from a flat-looking or poorly protractile nipple if he takes enough of the breast into his mouth. She may need extra help at first to get the baby to suckle in a good position. She needs to be patient, and to persist, but she can succeed and you will help her.
❏ Explain that her nipples will improve during pregnancy and when the baby begins to breastfeed. They may not look much longer but they should become more protractile.
❏ After the baby is born, give the mother extra help and support as early as possible. Try to get the baby to suckle in a good position from the first day. It may be easier to get the baby to suckle early, before the breasts become full.
❏ If the breast is engorged, the mother should express the milk until the breast is soft. This makes it easier for the baby to take enough of the breast into his mouth.
❏ If the baby does not succeed in taking the breast at first, reassure the mother that he will manage in the end. Make sure that she understands what she needs to do so that she can work at getting the baby to take the breast herself.
  She can express milk and feed it to the baby by cup while he learns to suckle.
❏ If it is acceptable to the couple, the woman's husband can suckle her breasts to help relieve engorgement and to make the nipple more protractile, before or after the baby is born.

The management is the same for poorly protractile and inverted nipples. However, a woman with inverted nipples needs more help for a longer time.

Nipple exercises and nipple shells

Some mothers may feel that they need to do something to improve their nipples.

In the past, health workers have taught mothers to do nipple stretching "exercises". However, it is not certain that exercises really make any difference. They can damage the nipple and sometimes cause uterine contractions (if oxytocin is released).

Health workers sometimes advise mothers to wear nipple shells. A nipple shell is a ring of glass or plastic which the mother wears under her clothes and which presses on the areola. The nipple is pushed out through the hole in the ring.

In some countries, mothers make nipple shells out of coconut shell, rings of grass, or cardboard. It is not certain that nipple shells really make any difference. However, if a mother wants to wear them, they may give her confidence that she can breastfeed.

5.6 "MY NIPPLES ARE TOO LONG"

Some women have nipples that are rather long. Long nipples may be a commoner cause of problems than inverted nipples.

If a nipple is long, then the baby may suck only on the nipple. He may not take enough of the breast tissue beneath the areola into his mouth. So:
- His tongue cannot press the lactiferous sinuses against the palate.
- He may not stimulate the oxytocin and prolactin reflexes.
- He may not get enough milk.
❏ Help the mother to get the baby to take more of the breast into his mouth.

5.7 "MY BABY REFUSES TO BREASTFEED"

This is important and may be serious.
- It can be a sign that the baby is ill—for example with an infection or brain damage.
- Sometimes the baby has a problem with his nose or mouth.
- More often, it is because breastfeeding has become a frustrating or unpleasant experience for the baby.

Sometimes mothers think that a baby is refusing when he is not.
- Some babies move their heads from side to side when they are rooting

for the nipple. This has been called *"homing"* behaviour. Some mothers think that the baby is saying "no"!

- Some babies find it more difficult than others to learn to suckle. The mother thinks that the baby does not want her milk.
- Some babies of about 5 months are easily distracted from breastfeeding, for example by noises.
- After the age of 1 year, some babies wean themselves.

The baby may be ill

If a baby has other signs of illness, for example vomiting, diarrhoea, sleepiness, jaundice or convulsions, he may be seriously ill.

❑ If you are worried, ask a more specialized health worker.

The baby may be too small and weak to suckle effectively

If he weighs less than 1,800 g:

❑ Help the mother to express her breastmilk and feed the EBM by cup until he can suckle more effectively (see Section 7.2).

The baby may have a problem with his nose or mouth

If he has a cold which is blocking his nose

❑ Show his mother how to clean his nose before each feed. She should take a piece of clean rag or absorbent paper and roll it into a point. She should push the point gently into the baby's nose, turn the point around, and withdraw it, cleaning first one nostril then the other. If the mucus is dry, she can wet the cloth with water.

If he has a sore mouth, for example, thrush

❑ Treat the baby with nystatin drops or gentian violet.

Some babies refuse to breastfeed when they are teething.

Breastfeeding is frustrating or unpleasant for the baby

Is there too much milk coming too fast?

When the baby starts to feed, milk pours out into his mouth and he chokes. This makes him frightened to feed from the breast. Milk sometimes pours out of the other breast too and the breasts may feel full between feeds. These are signs that the mother has an oversupply of milk and an active ejection reflex.

❑ Show the mother how to express some milk before each feed (see Section 10.1). Then the breasts are not so full and the milk does not flow so fast.

❑ Suggest that she offers the baby only one breast at each feed. Do not offer the other breast until the next feed. The breasts will be less stimulated and the supply of milk will adjust to the baby's needs.

❑ It may help to lie on her back to feed the baby. The milk cannot flow so fast upwards.

Has the baby been bottle fed?

If a baby has learnt to suck from a bottle he may refuse the breast.

– Did the baby have any bottle feeds before he started to breastfeed?
– Is the mother giving him bottle feeds at home?

Has the baby been separated from his mother?

If a baby is separated from his mother for some time after birth, or at any time afterwards, he may refuse to breastfeed.

– Was there a delay starting to feed in hospital?
– Does the mother leave the baby while she goes to work?
– Has she been away from him, for example because of illness?

Has the mother restricted breastfeeds?

Restricting feeds can lead to frustration and refusal.

– Has she tried to feed the baby only at certain times?
– Does she take him off the breast after a certain time?
– Has she made him wait for feeds?

Has the mother done something unusual and the baby is upset?

– It may happen if there has been a change in the family routine, such as going on a visit, or moving house. Perhaps his mother has not had time to feed him when he wanted to.
– Sometimes a baby refuses to breastfeed if the mother smells different— for example, if she eats a lot of garlic, or uses a new kind of soap or perfume, which she has not done before.
– A baby may refuse when his mother is ill, or menstruating, or if she has mastitis.

Is the baby getting very little breastmilk?

A baby who is not getting enough milk may become frustrated and refuse to suckle at the "empty" breast. The milk supply may decrease for a number of reasons (see Section 6.3).

Take the mother somewhere quiet and private and ask her to try to breastfeed the baby.

❑ Does the mother hold the baby close and show that she is happy with him? Sometimes refusing to suckle is the way that a baby reacts if the mother does not feel warmly towards him. Encourage her to talk about how she feels.

❑ If the baby suckles, is the position good? If the baby suckles in a poor position and no milk comes, he may pull away angrily and cry.

Bottle feeds may make a baby refuse the breast.

Teaching a baby who "refuses" to breastfeed

If possible, manage the mother and baby at home and visit them several times. Sometimes it may be necessary to admit them to hospital to give enough help.

❑ Keep mother and baby close together day and night. Do not let anybody else handle the baby. Let the mother pick him up and hold and cuddle him as much as possible. She should also sleep with the baby.

❑ Encourage the mother to offer the baby her breast whenever he seems willing to suckle, or when she feels her ejection reflex. She should not try to force him. Sometimes it helps to squeeze a little milk into the baby's mouth at the beginning of a feed.

❑ If the baby is very hungry, it may help to give him some EBM by cup and then put him to the breast when he is less frustrated. Some babies suckle better when they are sleepy.

❑ Make sure that the baby breastfeeds in a good position. Make sure that the mother understands how to get him to take enough breast into his mouth.

❑ Do not give any bottle feeds. If the baby is not taking enough milk from the breasts, let the mother express her milk every 2–3 hours and feed the EBM to the baby with a cup. Expressing helps to keep up her milk supply. If she cannot express enough, she can give the baby half-strength cow's milk feeds from a cup. Dilute feeds leave the baby hungry, so he is more willing to try to suckle. (However, check the baby's weight—do not let him starve.)

❑ Do not let the baby suck on a dummy.

5.8 "MY BREASTS LEAK MILK"

Some women find that their breasts leak milk during the first few weeks after delivery. This is often because they have a good supply of milk. Leaking is especially common when it is time for a feed, or if there is delay between feeds. Some women notice leaking whenever they think lovingly about their baby. It shows that their ejection reflex is active. Women who go out to work may find leaking very troublesome and embarrassing.

It is difficult to stop leaking completely. However, it usually stops by itself after a few weeks when the breasts become softer.

Advising a mother whose breasts leak milk

❑ Reassure her that it should stop in time, even though she will continue to produce plenty of milk.

❑ Show her how she can put clean pieces of rag inside her clothes to soak up the milk. She should change the rags frequently and wash them thoroughly. Small pieces of towelling are very suitable; so are pieces of sanitary towels if she can afford to buy them.

❑ At work, she can express some milk. Keep it to give to the baby later. If she cannot keep it she must throw it away. Her breasts will make plenty more.

5.9 "THERE IS BLOOD IN MY MILK"

Some women notice a little blood in their milk or in the baby's vomit. There is no nipple fissure or sore.

❑ Advise the mother to keep on breastfeeding. The condition is usually harmless and it will soon stop.

CHAPTER SIX

Later problems and continuing to breastfeed

Encourage mothers to continue with frequent, unrestricted breastfeeding by day and night. Many will have no difficulties. However, there are certain problems that occur most commonly after a baby is a few weeks old.

6.1 "I DO NOT HAVE ENOUGH MİLK"

This is one of the commonest reasons that mothers give for wanting to feed their baby on a bottle, or on cow's milk or cereal porridge too early. Many health workers accept what a mother says and advise her to give supplements. However, often the mother has plenty of breastmilk and only lacks confidence that it is enough. Sometimes the baby is not getting the milk, even though she can produce enough. Sometimes the supply has decreased because the baby is not removing the milk. Almost all mothers *can* produce enough milk if they want to, and if the baby suckles in a good position, and breastfeeds often enough.

First you must decide what the problem is.

❑ Ask the mother: "What makes you feel that you do not have enough milk?"

She may complain that the baby seems unsatisfied because he:
- Cries more than the family expects.
- Wants to feed more often than the mother has time for.
- Takes a long time over feeds.
- Fusses at the breast or refuses to feed.

- Sucks his fingers.
- Takes bottle feeds and sleeps longer.

She may worry that:
- Her breasts do not feel full as soon as the baby is born.
- Her breasts feel softer than they did before.
- Milk has stopped dripping out.

❏ Ask her who is advising her and if someone is telling her that she does not have enough breastmilk.

Figure 18. Breastfeeding at 3 months.

Then you must try to decide:
- If the baby is taking enough breastmilk or not.
- What the problem is.
- How you can help the mother.

6.2 HOW TO DECIDE IF A BABY IS TAKING ENOUGH BREASTMILK

The wetness test

Ask the mother how often the baby urinates, or has a wet nappy. He should urinate six or more times a day and the urine should be colourless or pale yellow.
- If the baby breastfeeds and has nothing else, and if he urinates six times in 24 hours, then he is taking enough breastmilk.
- If his mother is giving him water or other drinks, then this test cannot help you. The water will make urine, even if the baby does not get enough milk.

A baby who is growing well is getting enough milk.

The weight check

Weigh the baby and check his weight gain on a growth chart (see Figure 19). Weigh the baby every month or two routinely. Weigh him every week if you are worried about him. When you see a baby, make sure that you ask to see the chart.

A healthy baby should gain between half and one kilo per month— or a minimum of 125 g each week. A child's growth line should follow the printed reference curve on the chart. The child's line may be above or below the reference curve—but it must be about the same shape.

If the baby's growth line follows the reference curve
He is gaining weight well, so he is having enough breastmilk.
❏ Reassure the mother that she has enough breastmilk and advise her not to start a supplement or solid foods.

Explaining that what she notices is normal, and building her confidence, may be all that is necessary.

If the baby is fussing at the breast and does not seem satisfied:
❏ Check the suckling position and feeding pattern.
❏ Think of other reasons why the baby may be crying (see Section 6.4) and discuss them with the mother.

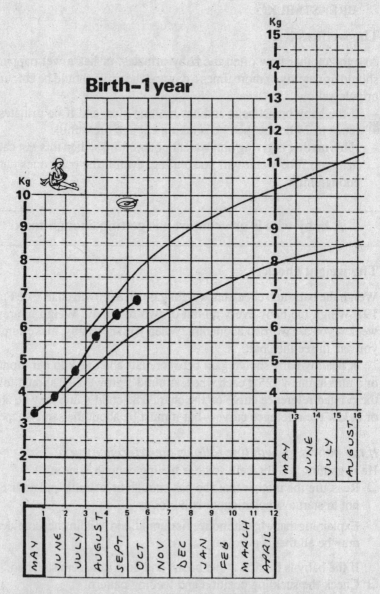

Figure 19. Growth chart showing satisfactory weight gain. The baby's growth line is following the reference curve.

If the baby's growth line rises faster than the reference curve
Breastfed babies may gain weight faster than the reference curve in the first few months. This is normal. It shows that their mothers have plenty of milk and that breastmilk is the best food. Fast weight gain on breastmilk alone usually slows down after about 4–5 months.

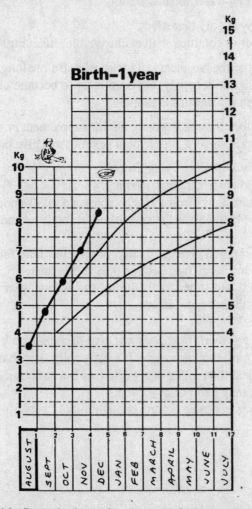

Figure 20. Growth chart showing weight increasing too fast.
The baby's growth line is rising faster than the reference curve.

A baby who continues to gain more than one kilo per month may be becoming overweight, which can be unhealthy.

❏ Ask the mother if she is giving the child anything other than breastmilk. A baby may become overweight if his mother feeds him extra cow's milk or solids that he does not need. She may feed him extra if he cries a lot, or if he wants to suckle a lot.

If the baby is only breastfed:
❏ Advise her to continue with exclusive breastfeeding.

Explain that she has plenty of breastmilk. Before long, the baby will outgrow her milk supply. He is unlikely to become unhealthily overweight on breastmilk alone.

If the mother is already giving a milk supplement or solids:
❏ Advise her to stop the supplement or solids and give breastmilk only.

If the baby is already 6 months old:
❏ She should continue breastfeeding.
❏ She can start to give fruit and vegetables and *small* amounts of cereals, so that the baby learns the taste of other foods and he learns to take solids.
❏ Advise her not to give extra milk, or sweet or fatty foods, which are very rich in energy (see Section 9.5) at this time.
❏ She should add other foods during the second year as the baby's growth becomes more steady.

If the baby's growth line does not rise fast enough
He is not gaining enough weight. If a baby gains less than half a kilo in a month, or less than 125 g in a week, this is a serious sign.
– The baby may be ill or abnormal.
– The baby may not be getting enough milk.

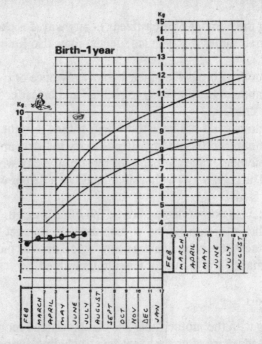

Figure 21. Growth chart showing weight increasing too slowly. The baby's growth line is almost flat and does not follow the reference curve.

6.3 A BABY WHO DOES NOT GAIN ENOUGH WEIGHT

The baby may be ill or abnormal

The baby may have an infection, for example in the chest or the urine. He may have a congenital abnormality, such as a heart problem, or a mental handicap.

❏ If you think that the baby might have a medical problem, treat him or refer him to a more specialized health worker.

The baby is not getting enough milk

The problem may be one of the following:

1. The mother does not breastfeed the baby often enough
Breastfeeding less than 5–6 times a day is a common reason for a poor milk supply.

65

Restricting the number of breastfeeds in any way, for example feeding only at certain times ("scheduled" feeds) may also limit the supply of breastmilk.

- Some mothers breastfeed their babies only once or twice a day.
- Some mothers feel too busy to pick up and breastfeed a baby every time he cries.
- Some mothers do not breastfeed their babies at night.
- Some mothers miss out breastfeeds to try to "save up" their milk.
- Some mothers leave the baby for most of the day while they are at work. The baby stays with a small child or a helper who gives only watery feeds.
- Some babies do not demand to be fed often enough. Their mothers think that they are "good", but they do not get enough milk. Sometimes these babies have a neurological or other medical problem which makes it difficult for them to breastfeed.

What to do

❏ Discuss with the mother how she can breastfeed more often. If she breastfeeds more often for a few days, including during the night, her milk supply will increase and the baby should start to gain weight.

❏ Perhaps she can take the baby with her to work, or she can ask a helper to bring the baby to her so that she can breastfeed. Perhaps she can feed the baby more at night and express her milk for him to have during the day (see Section 6.6).

❏ If the baby does not demand to be fed she should wake him up and breastfeed him about every 3 hours.

❏ Advise her that it is much better for the baby if he takes only breastmilk. She should try not to give a supplement before the baby is at least 4 months of age. Supplements may make the baby ill and her breastmilk may decrease further.

2. The baby does not want to suckle for long enough

Some babies suckle for only a few seconds and then they fall asleep. This is especially likely if a baby wears a lot of clothes when he feeds. After a short time, he wakes up crying because he is hungry again. His mother thinks that she does not have enough milk.

What to do

❏ Discuss with the mother how she can make the baby feed at each breast for at least 5–10 minutes.
❏ If he goes to sleep during a feed she should stroke him on the cheek to wake him up gently.
❏ She should not wrap the baby in many clothes when he is feeding.

If a baby does not suckle enough, the supply of milk decreases.

---

3. The mother restricts the length of a breastfeed

A mother may have learnt that a baby should only feed for 5–10 minutes. She takes the baby off the breast after a short time, before he has finished. A slow feeding baby may not get enough milk, especially the fat-rich hindmilk. He may seem to be hungry; he may want to suckle often; but he may fail to gain weight.

What to do

❏ Explain to the mother that some babies are slow feeders and take 20–30 minutes or more. She should let her baby continue until he stops suckling by himself. If she is busy, this can give her a chance to sit, or lie down and rest for a short time.

4. The mother started supplements too early

Some mothers give supplements from an early age—either formula, cow's milk, cereal, juice, teas or other drinks. The supplement fills the baby's stomach, he suckles less at the breast and the breastmilk supply decreases.

A baby may sleep longer after a cow's milk or cereal feed. He may not cry with hunger so quickly. Many mothers think that this is a sign that the baby needed the supplement, and that they do not have enough breastmilk. The real reason is that cow's milk and cereal take longer to digest than breastmilk (see Section 3.6).

What to do

❏ Explain the dangers of supplements (see Section 9.3) and advise the mother to breastfeed exclusively.

❏ She should breastfeed very often including at night for a few days to increase her supply of breastmilk.

❏ Explain that the baby may be hungry more often, but if he gains weight he is getting enough breastmilk.

5. The baby suckles in a poor position

If a baby suckles in a poor position he does not remove the breastmilk effectively and the supply decreases.

What to do

❏ Help the mother to improve the suckling position.

6. The mother has a poor ejection reflex

This may be commoner in urban areas than in rural areas. If a mother is anxious, or in pain, or lonely, or embarrassed, her feelings may hinder her ejection reflex so that her milk does not flow well. She can produce enough breastmilk but her baby does not get it (see Section 2.4). If the milk is not removed her supply will decrease.

Ask the mother:
"What do you feel in your breasts when you start to feed?"

If she says that she feels "squeezing" or tightness, then her ejection reflex is working.

If she does not feel the squeezing, then she *may* have a problem with the reflex. However, it is possible for a woman to have an active ejection reflex but not to feel it.

What to do

❏ Reassure the mother that she can make plenty of milk and that she can breastfeed the baby.

❏ Spend some time talking with her and try to find out if she has any special worries. You may not be able to solve all her problems but discussing them may help her.

❑ Help her to sit or lie down in a relaxed position when she feeds the baby. It may help her to take a warm drink before she tries to feed, for example a lactogogue (see Section 10.5). A good laugh or a good cry may also help her to relax.

❑ Make sure that breastfeeding is not painful—check the baby's sucking position.

❑ Suggest that if she does feel the squeezing in her breasts she can feed the baby then because the milk may be easier for him to get. If she does this a few times it helps the reflex to work when the baby wants to suckle.

A mother who lacks confidence can doubt her milk away.

---

7. The mother lacks confidence

Some mothers do not believe that they can breastfeed. They may not know what to expect. They may lack social support, or their family or friends may encourage them to bottle feed.

What to do

❑ Reassure her that she can breastfeed and help her to feel that it is worthwhile to try.

❑ Encourage her to ask questions and explain that what she experiences is normal.

❑ Try to support her to resist the advice of her friends and family. Try to find somebody sympathetic who can visit her at home to continue to support and reassure her. If there is a breastfeeding counsellor or a mother-to-mother support group in the area, introduce her to them.

8. The mother is not enthusiastic about breastfeeding

Sometimes a mother does not really want to breastfeed. She may not enjoy breastfeeding and she may not be willing to make an effort. She may want to be able to leave the baby with someone else, or her friends or family may have persuaded her that artificial feeding is better. You may feel that she does not want the help that you offer to succeed.

What to do

❑ Explain again the advantages of breastfeeding and the risks of artificial feeding. Emphasize the advantages to her, such as losing any weight that she has gained, and saving money and trouble.

❑ Try to share your enthusiasm with her and make her feel good about breastfeeding so that she wants to try for a few months anyway.

Keeping mother and babies together from immediately after delivery to bond might prevent this problem.

9. The mother is undernourished

Mothers who are moderately undernourished can produce enough breastmilk. Mothers who are severely malnourished may produce less milk with less fat than well-nourished mothers. But their breastmilk is still the best food for the baby. The baby may have to suckle more often to stimulate the secretion of more prolactin to keep up the supply of breastmilk, and the mother's body stores may become depleted. Some babies may outgrow the milk supply and stop gaining weight a few weeks earlier than usual, especially if they suckle less for any reason.

However, undernourished mothers usually do not complain that they have too little milk or that the baby is crying. Often they have to work very hard and also find it difficult to feed their babies often enough.

What to do

❑ Look carefully for undernourished mothers who do not complain.

❑ The most important thing to do is to help mothers to eat more themselves, for their own health and strength as well as for the baby.

❑ Weigh their babies regularly and watch for signs of poor growth.

❑ Try to avoid recommending early supplements. Remember that undernourished mothers are usually poor. It may be even more difficult for them to find a suitable supplement for their babies than to eat more themselves. If they give a supplement, the baby may breastfeed less and the supply of breastmilk will decrease.

10. The mother is taking an oestrogen-containing contraceptive pill

The "combination" pills may reduce milk production.

What to do

❑ Help the mother to obtain a different contraceptive (see Section 8.5).
❑ Help her to build up her milk supply (see Section 10.5). Reassure her that her milk will come back when she changes her contraceptive.

11. The mother really has a poor supply

Perhaps 1% of women really have difficulty producing enough milk for their babies.

What to do

If the baby is not gaining enough weight, and you think that the mother might really not be able to produce enough milk:

❑ Check that he is not sick or abnormal.
❑ Make sure that he is suckling in a good position and do all that you can to help the mother to increase her milk supply.
❑ It may help if she feeds the baby twice from each breast at each feed. She can feed him from both breasts, and then again from one or both sides.
❑ If all this fails, she may have to give the baby a supplement of cow's milk. She should give it with a cup and not a bottle.
❑ Encourage her to continue to give as much breastmilk as possible and to let the baby suckle before she gives the supplement.

Perhaps 1% of women cannot make enough milk.

6.4 "MY BABY CRIES TOO MUCH"

A baby cries when there is something wrong. Crying is his only way to ask for help. If he is dirty or hungry, his mother usually knows what to do. But babies also cry when they are lonely, uncomfortable, or afraid. Some babies seem to cry more than others.

A mother may think that her child is ill or that her breastmilk is not good. She may ask you to help her to decide what to do. Sometimes the pattern of the baby's crying can help you to understand the problem.

Crying because of illness

If a baby is ill, his crying pattern changes. A baby who did not cry much before suddenly starts to cry a lot—especially if he is in pain, for example with an ear infection.

How to help a baby who may be ill
❑ Examine him carefully and try to decide what illness he has.
❑ Treat him or refer him to a more specialized health worker.

Crying because he does not get enough milk

A baby may seem content and go to sleep immediately after a breastfeed. He then wakes and cries for another feed after an hour or so. If a baby cries in this way, then it is possible that he is not getting enough milk.

How to help a mother whose baby is crying with hunger
❑ Weigh the baby to find out if he is getting enough milk or not.
❑ Look for all the causes of a poor milk supply (see Section 6.3). Often the problem is that the mother does not feed the baby often enough because she is too busy.
❑ Check the baby's feeding position—he may not be getting the milk efficiently.
❑ Discuss with the mother how she can build up her milk supply. Help her to find a way to feed the baby more often. Advise her about other ways to increase her milk (see Section 10.4). It may help to explain that if the baby breastfeeds more often and the milk supply increases, the baby may be more content.

Crying because the baby has temporarily outgrown the milk supply

Some experts call this a "lactation crisis". It happens most often when a baby is 2–3 months old. The baby suddenly starts to cry and to demand to be breastfed frequently. He seems to be more hungry than before. Sometimes his growth line flattens and he passes green stools.

What has happened is that the baby has grown faster than his mother's milk supply. If she breastfeeds more often for a few days, the milk supply increases and becomes enough for the baby again. The stools become yellow again in a day or two.

Sometimes, in very hot weather, a baby may start crying and demanding to suckle because he is more thirsty than usual. Many mothers become very worried when their babies cry more. They may start to give a supplement.

How to help a mother with a lactation crisis

❑ Discuss with her that it is better not to give a supplement. If she does, her milk supply will not increase.

❑ Explain that if the baby feeds more often for 3–8 days, she will have enough breastmilk again.

❑ If the baby is thirsty, breastmilk will satisfy his thirst. It is not necessary to give drinks of water.

❑ Discuss other ways to increase her breastmilk supply (see Section 10.5).

Crying because he does not get enough hindmilk

Sometimes a mother takes her baby off the first breast before he has finished, or to make him feed from the second breast. The baby may not get enough fat-rich hindmilk. He may take too much foremilk and get too much lactose, which can upset him.

Some of these babies have loose green stools and a poor weight gain. Some grow well, but they cry and want to feed often, or for a very long time at each feed. Either way, the mother usually has plenty of breastmilk.

❑ Suggest that the mother lets the baby finish feeding on the first breast before she offers the second. He may want little or none from the second breast.

Crying is not always due to hunger.

73

Figure 22. This mother thinks that if she feeds the baby a supplement, he will stop crying.

Substances in the mother's food

Small amounts of substances in a mother's food (e.g. cow's milk or coffee) may pass unchanged into her breastmilk. Occasionally these may upset the baby and make him cry. Almost any food *can* do this so it is not possible to advise a mother about foods to avoid. Sometimes a mother notices that the baby is upset when she eats something unusual. Sometimes it helps if the mother stops drinking cow's milk.

❏ She should stop taking milk, including milk in tea or food, for 2 weeks.

Figure 23. She fed him from a bottle and this is what happened. He developed diarrhoea and malnutrition. He is too weak to cry now.

If cow's milk is the cause

The baby will cry less. The mother should continue to avoid taking milk until the baby is about 4 months old.

If cow's milk is not the cause

The baby will continue to cry. The mother can take milk again if she wishes.

Be careful about advising a woman to stop taking milk if she herself is undernourished. Make sure that she can eat extra food of a different kind, such as beans.

Babies who cry more than usual

Some babies cry more than others because they need to be held, carried and comforted more than other babies. They may like to suckle for comfort (see Section 2.9), but they do not really need more milk.

Crying that occurs very soon *after* a feed is not due to hunger. The baby may behave as if he is hungry, for example by sucking his fists. If the mother holds the baby, he may demand to be nursed and "root" for the breast because he can smell her milk; but he is not really hungry.

Often the mother decides that the baby is hungry and that she does not have enough milk. Many mothers give their babies a supplement. About half of the babies cry less; about half of them continue to cry, or they cry more.

Some babies cry mainly at a certain time of day, for example in the evening. The baby may cry every day at that time until he is 3–4 months old. Doctors may call it "colic" because some babies pull up their knees when they cry as if they have abdominal pain.

How to help the mother of a baby who cries more than usual
❑ Weigh the baby and check his growth line. Most babies who cry in this way are growing well.

❑ Check the baby's suckling position and if necessary help the mother to improve it.

❑ Explain to the mother that:
   – The baby is not ill.
   – There is no problem with her milk. The baby is not hungry and she should not stop breastfeeding. Most babies who cry a lot grow well. Your weight check should reassure her.
   – This kind of crying usually stops when the baby is 3–4 months old.
   – The baby does not need milk supplements or food. Sometimes cow's milk makes the baby worse.
   – It is better not to waste money on gripe water or other medicines. They do not always help and they can be harmful.

❑ Explain that babies usually cry less if they are carried and held and fed "on demand". "Comfort" feeding at the breast is safe for the baby but bottles are not safe.

- Can she carry and comfort the baby more?
- Can she put him to the breast more often?

❑ Sometime it is easier for another person, who does not have breastmilk, to calm the baby, for example, the grandmother or the father.
- Sometimes it helps to carry a baby face down over one arm so that there is pressure on his stomach. Rhythmic movements may help.
- The father can carry the baby upright against his chest, with the baby's head against his throat, talking softly. Many babies are quietened by a man's low voice. This is one way in which a father can really help a mother.

Figure 24. If a baby cries more than usual, it may help to carry the baby face down over one arm.

Figure 25. Sometimes it is easier for a father to quieten a crying baby.

6.5 "I HAVE TO GO BACK TO WORK"

One of the commonest reasons that mothers give for not breastfeeding is that they have to work.

Women have always worked, especially in their child-bearing years. Finding a way to care for children and to work has always been a problem. When people say "work" they often mean paid employment in town. But it is also difficult to work in the fields at the same time as breastfeeding.

Women need control over their own time so that they can attend to a baby when they want to. This is why breastfeeding is easier for a woman who is self-employed, for example, if she sells in the market. It is also easier if her work is in or near her home.

The long-term solution

Social change and legislation are needed to:
- Give women longer paid maternity leave. They should not have to return to work before a baby can safely start supplements, that is, when he is 4 months old.
- Provide "creches" at places of employment so that women can take their babies and breastfeed during nursing breaks.
- Arrange working hours, especially shift work, so that it is possible for women to breastfeed.

Health workers especially need help to breastfeed.

Health workers who are also mothers

Women doctors, nurses and other health workers may also be mothers. If they are to encourage and help other women to breastfeed, they must be able to breastfeed themselves and set an example.

In many places it is health workers who are the first to bottle feed. This is because of the problems that they face when they return to work after delivery. The hours of their shifts can make breastfeeding very difficult. Yet they cannot hope to teach other mothers to do what they cannot do themselves.

Creches in health institutions

The first step in a campaign to increase breastfeeding may be to provide a creche for the babies of the women staff who work in health institutions. It need not be very difficult or expensive and there are some countries in Africa where this has already started, for example Mozambique.

How to advise a working mother now

Discuss different possibilities. Can she take her baby with her to work, or go home to feed him during breaks, or ask someone to bring the baby to her at work to breastfeed?

If not, for example, if her home is too far from her work place, if there are no creches, or if the buses are too crowded, she can still give her baby the benefit of breastfeeding.

To do this, she should:

- ❏ *Breastfeed exclusively and frequently for the whole maternity leave.* This gives the baby the benefit of breastfeeding and it builds up the mother's milk supply. The first 2 months are the most important.

- ❏ *Avoid starting other feeds before she really needs to.* Discourage her from thinking: "I shall have to go back to work in 8 weeks so I might as well bottle feed straight away". Some working mothers think that they have to get the baby "used" to artificial feeds. That is not necessary. She can wait until the last day or two before she goes back to work. She should leave just enough time to teach the carer who will look after the baby.

- ❏ *Continue to breastfeed at night, in the early morning, and at any other time that she is at home.*
  - This helps her to keep up her milk supply.
  - It gives the baby the benefit of breastmilk, even if she decides to give him one or two artificial feeds during the day.
  - Many babies "learn" to suckle more at night and get most of the milk that they need then. They sleep more and need less milk during the day.

- ❏ *Learn to express milk soon after the baby is born* so that she can do it easily (see Section 10.1).

- ❏ *Express milk before she goes to work* and leave it for the carer to give to the baby. Explain to the mother that she needs to:
  - Leave herself enough time to express her milk in a relaxed way. She may need to wake up half an hour earlier than at other times. (If she hurries she may find that she cannot express enough milk.)
  - Breastfeed the baby as soon as she wakes up, before she gets up.
  - Express as much milk as she can into a very clean cup or jar. Many mothers find that they can express 400–500 ml even after the baby has fed. Some mothers report 800 ml or more. Leave $\frac{1}{2}$–1 cup for each feed that the baby will need while she is out.
  - Cover the cup of expressed milk with a clean cloth or saucer.
  - Leave the milk in the coolest place that she can find—in a refrigerator if she has one, or just in the shade. She does not need to boil the milk or reheat it for the baby. Heat destroys the anti-infective factors.

EBM stays in good condition longer than cow's milk because of the anti-infective substances in it. Germs do not start growing in EBM for at least 8 hours, even in a hot climate and outside the refrigerator. It is safe to give to the baby at least throughout one working day.

❑ *If she decides to use cow's milk she should:*
- Boil ⅓ cup of water and ⅔ cup of cow's milk to make 1 cup (200 ml) of feed. Add 1 level spoonful of sugar.
- Leave ½–1 cup of mixture for each feed that the baby will need while she is out.
- Leave the mixture in a clean, covered container.
- From the age of 6 months the baby should be taking weaning foods (see Chapter 9). She can also give full strength cow's milk and also drinks of water.

❑ *If she decides to use formula she should:*
- Measure the powder for a feed into 1 clean cup or glass.
- Measure the water to make up the feed into another clean glass.
- Cover them both with a clean cloth or put them in a covered pan.
- Teach the baby's carer to mix the milk powder and water when she is going to feed the baby. She must mix and use the formula immediately because it spoils very quickly after it is mixed.

Figure 26. Water and powder measured and covered.

Note: There are many different ways to leave milk for a baby. These are satisfactory methods. She may find a different method that is better for her in her situation.

❑ *She must teach the carer properly and carefully.* She should:
  - Teach the carer to feed the baby with a cup and not to use a bottle (see Section 10.7). Cups are cleaner and they do not satisfy the baby's need to suck. So when the mother comes home the baby wants to suckle at the breast and this stimulates the breastmilk supply.
  - Teach the carer to give all the feed at one time. She must not keep it to give later and she must not give a small amount every now and again.

❑ *While at work, the mother should express her milk.*
  If she does not express, her milk supply may decrease. Expressing also keeps her breasts comfortable and reduces leaking.
- If she works somewhere where she can use a refrigerator, she can keep the EBM there. She should carry a clean jar with a lid to store the milk and take it home for the baby.

(a) *Massaging the breast gently towards the nipple.*

(b) *Pressing behind the nipple to express milk (see Section 10.1).*

Figure 27. Expressing breastmilk to leave for the baby.

– If she cannot keep the EBM she should throw it away. The baby has not lost anything and her breasts will make more milk.

Mothers can express milk at work to keep up their supply.

If you are a health worker, make sure that your patients know and see how you manage. Then they can follow your example.

Many mothers have continued to breastfeed their babies and keep them healthy while they continued in full-time employment. And some of them are nurses and doctors.

CHAPTER SEVEN

Breastfeeding in special situations

7.1 FULL-TERM TWINS

Most mothers have enough breastmilk to feed twins. Difficulties arise because it is hard work to look after two babies at the same time. Mothers may need a lot of support and encouragement to believe that they can breastfeed them both. They may need help to find out the best way to do it.

Some mothers feed both twins at the same time; some feed first one twin and then the other. Sometimes each twin always feeds from one special side; sometimes they feed from each breast alternately. The best method probably depends partly on whether she has someone to help her—such as an older daughter.

How to help a mother of twins

❑ Reassure the mother that she does have enough milk for two babies. Remind her that more suckling makes more milk, so if two babies suckle there will be enough for two. Many women have enough for more than two babies.

❑ Help her to find the best method for her and her babies. Each mother is different. One way to breastfeed twins together is to hold the babies with their bodies and legs going under the mother's arms, as in Figure 28.

❑ Talk to her husband and discuss with him how he can help his wife to manage two babies. Talk to other family members about how they can help with other work so that she is free to breastfeed the babies.

❏ Sometimes one twin is weaker than the other. Encourage her to make sure that the weaker twin gets enough breastmilk. If necessary, she can express milk for him.

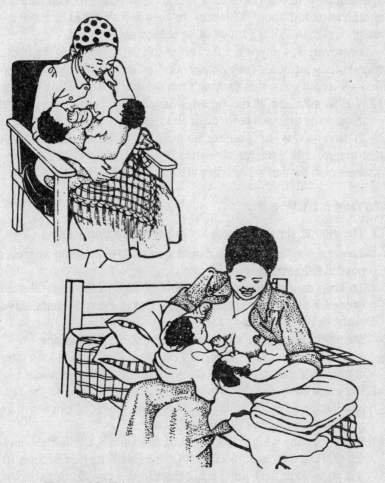

Figure 28. Two ways to hold twins for breastfeeding.

7.2 LOW BIRTH WEIGHT (LBW) BABIES—SMALL TWINS AND SMALL SINGLETONS

It is possible to feed almost all LBW babies on their mother's milk. Fresh breastmilk prevents many infections. Mothers who feed and care for their own babies are less likely to abandon or abuse them. When necessary, breastmilk can be fortified with calcium and other nutrients.

Babies are able to suckle and swallow from about 34 weeks gestational age. But they may not be able to suckle well enough to feed themselves completely until about 37 weeks, or they weigh 1,800 g. Babies who weigh less than 1,600 g may not be able to suckle at all.

However, it is important for babies to start suckling at the breast as soon as they are able. They do *not* need to "learn" to suck from a bottle first—we now know that sucking from a bottle is more tiring for a small baby than suckling at the breast. Also, bottle feeding causes nipple confusion and makes it more difficult to get the baby to breastfeed later.

When a baby is born preterm, his mother's milk contains more protein than mature milk. Preterm babies need extra protein, and they grow better on their own mother's preterm milk than on donated mature milk.

To feed a LBW baby

❑ The mother should express her milk (see Section 10.1).

– To get a good supply, she should start hand expressing as soon as possible after delivery.

– To keep up a good supply, she should express as much as she can every time the baby needs to feed—that is every 3 hours, day and night, or eight times in 24 hours.

– She should not leave a long interval between expressions.

– If she expresses only 1–2 times a day, or if she leaves a long interval at night without expressing, her milk supply will decrease.

❑ Babies who weigh less than 1,600 g usually need to be fed by nasogastric tube. The milk must flow down the tube from a syringe by gravity. It should not be forced down.

❑ When the baby weighs 1,600 g, and can swallow, the mother can feed the expressed breastmilk (EBM) from a small cup (see Section 10.4). It is possible to feed very small babies from a cup. Some experienced workers have found that cup feeding can be safer than tube feeding.

❑ When the baby is 1,600 g, he can also start trying to suckle. This helps him to develop the ability to suckle and it stimulates the milk-producing reflexes. Suckling may also help the baby to digest the milk and to grow faster.

Figure 29. Feeding a low birth weight baby EBM from a cup.

❏ Help him to take the breast into his mouth in a good position. Probably a LBW baby can feed himself completely sooner if he suckles in a good position from the beginning. At first, a LBW baby suckles a few times and then rests, and then suckles again. Let him stay on the breast while he rests.

Let a small baby suckle as soon as he is able.

❏ After the baby has suckled as much as he can, the mother should express her milk. Then she should feed him a measured amount of the EBM with a small cup.

❏ Keep the baby warm. Small babies easily become cold, even in a hot climate. A cold baby burns up all his food trying to keep warm and he does not gain weight. Discuss with the mother how she can keep the baby warm. One good way is to let the baby sleep with her, wrapped in the same blanket. Another way is to carry the baby next to her body inside her clothes between her breasts (see Figure 30).

❏ Weigh the baby regularly to make sure that he gains weight.

Figure 30. Keeping a LBW baby warm next to his mother's body.

7.3 HOW MUCH MILK TO GIVE BY TUBE OR CUP

First day of the baby's life

Give 60 ml per kilo of body weight per day. Divide the total into eight feeds and feed the baby every 3 hours.

Second day

Give 80 ml per kilo of body weight.

Third day

Give 100 ml per kilo of body weight.

Fourth to seventh day

Increase the daily total by 20 ml per kilo of body weight per day.

From the eighth day

Give 200 ml per kilo of body weight per day. Continue with that amount until the baby weighs 1,800 g and he is feeding himself from the breast, and he is continuing to gain weight.

Before the mother can produce enough milk

Most mothers can produce enough breastmilk within a day or two if they have help and support. Mothers who have breastfed before usually produce milk on the first day. If this is their first baby, milk takes longer to come. If they use a good technique to express milk, most mothers can produce 200–300 ml per day by the third day, and increasing amounts thereafter.

LBW babies need to start feeding within the first 6 hours of life to prevent low blood sugar, or hypoglycaemia.

Sometimes for the first few feeds it may be necessary to use EBM from another mother who has more milk than her own baby needs. Some LBW babies may need 5% glucose intravenously or by nasogastric tube.

❑ Make every effort to feed a baby on his own mother's milk as soon as possible.

❑ If she produces a very small amount, make sure that it is given to her baby, even if you have to give something else as well. A small amount of colostrum helps to prevent infection.

❑ The mother must know that her milk is given to her baby.

Using EBM from another woman

If HIV infection (AIDS) is a problem, you may not feel able to give a baby fresh milk from another mother ("donated" EBM). Probably any risk is very low, but we do not yet know enough to be certain.

❑ Pasteurize the donated EBM at 56°C for 30 minutes. This is enough to kill the AIDS virus.

❑ If you cannot pasteurize the EBM, boil it for a short time.

– If you cannot use donated EBM and you have to use formula or cow's milk, give it by tube or cup and never by bottle.

– If HIV infection is not a problem, give the donated EBM fresh as soon as possible after the woman expresses it.

7.4 EXTRA SUPPORT FOR MOTHERS OF LBW BABIES

Mothers who deliver small babies, and who deliver before time, need extra encouragement and support. They feel worried about the baby; they may feel that they have failed to bring home a strong baby. Try to make sure that they have support at home and that they eat enough themselves. A mother-to-mother group or a counsellor may be able to help.

It may take longer than usual for their milk supply to build up. A small baby may not be able to suckle and stimulate the nipple strongly. But he needs the protection of breastmilk even more than a big baby.

❑ Encourage the mother to believe that:
  - She *can* breastfeed her small baby.
  - Her milk is the best food, especially for such a small weak baby. She is doing the best thing for her baby if she expresses her milk and feeds it to him.
  - She is doing well if she expresses even a very small amount of colostrum. Babies only need a small amount of milk at first.

❑ Explain that:
  - Expressing will help her milk supply to build up.
  - It will become easier when the baby is big enough to suckle and stimulate the nipple himself.

❑ Let her stay near her baby in hospital and do as much as she is able to for him. This helps her to have a good milk supply.
  - Touching and holding her baby helps her to feel loving towards him and to bond with him.
  - If she can look at the baby, or hold him on her lap while she expresses, it will help her milk to flow.
  - If a mother is separated from her small baby at this time she finds it difficult to bond with him. Breastfeeding is more likely to fail and she is more likely to abandon or abuse the baby.

❑ Encourage mothers to help and support each other and to express their milk together. This helps their milk to flow.

Let mothers do as much as possible for their LBW babies.

7.5 CLEFT LIP OR PALATE

A mother whose baby has a cleft lip or palate also needs extra encouragement and support. A cleft lip can usually be corrected when the baby is about 3 months old. A cleft palate is usually corrected when the baby is about 1 year old. The problem is to feed him so that he grows and becomes strong enough for the operation.

If the cleft is of the lips and gums only, the baby should be able to breastfeed successfully.

❑ Encourage his mother to try.
❑ Help the baby to suckle in a good position. If he takes enough of the breast into his mouth, the breast may close over the cleft so that he can suckle well.

If the cleft involves the palate, suckling is more difficult. Some babies with this problem learn to breastfeed completely. They are more likely to succeed if the cleft is on *one side only*. It is more difficult if the cleft is on *both sides*. The baby may seem to choke sometimes and milk may leak through the nose.

❑ Encourage the mother to let the baby try, and give her all the support that you can.
❑ The baby may choke less if she holds him in a more upright position.
❑ Some babies need to be fed EBM by tube or with a cup until they are able to suckle well enough at the breast. Some babies need to be fed through a special long teat. However, a baby who sucks through a teat may lose interest in trying to suckle from the breast.

7.6 TONGUE TIE

Occasionally, a baby with tongue tie cannot put his tongue far enough forward to remove milk effectively. If a baby is having problems, it may be necessary to ask the doctor to cut the frenulum beneath the tongue.

However, many babies have slight tongue tie but they can suckle perfectly well.

7.7 A BABY WITH JAUNDICE

Early jaundice

It is quite common for a baby to look yellow, or *jaundiced*, in the first week of life. Jaundice usually starts on the second or third day and clears by the tenth day. It is commonest in LBW babies, but it often occurs in larger babies too. Jaundice is usually due to slight immaturity of the baby's liver. Sometimes there is a problem with the baby's blood. Treatment is necessary only if the jaundice is severe.

Early jaundice is *not* a reason to stop breastfeeding. In fact, jaundice is partly caused by the baby not getting enough breastmilk. The baby may not have started to breastfeed soon enough. He may not breastfeed often enough, or for long enough.

Colostrum helps to clear meconium and helps to prevent jaundice. If a baby gets enough breastmilk, it can help to clear early jaundice. But giving glucose water, plain water or other supplements does *not* help. These drinks interfere with breastfeeding and can make jaundice worse.

Sometimes a baby with jaundice is sleepy and does not want to suckle often or strongly enough. You need to help these babies to take enough breastmilk.

❑ If the baby is suckling well, continue to breastfeed him frequently, whenever he is hungry, by day and at night.

❑ If the baby is sleepy and not suckling enough, the mother may need to express her milk and give the EBM by cup every 3 hours.

❑ If the baby is having EBM anyway because he is LBW, and you are measuring it, give him 20% extra.

❑ A baby should continue to breastfeed even if the jaundice is severe and he has to have treatment (usually light therapy).

Glucose water does not help to clear jaundice.

Prolonged jaundice

Sometimes jaundice starts at the end of the first week of life and continues for several weeks. This can be due to serious illness in the baby.

Often, prolonged jaundice is not serious but is due to a reaction to substances in the mother's milk. The baby remains well and gains weight. If the mother continues breastfeeding, the jaundice clears after 3–10 weeks, with no treatment.

If the jaundice is very severe the doctor may need to diagnose whether it is due to serious illness or not. They may ask the mother to stop breastfeeding the baby for 48 hours. If the jaundice is due to the breastmilk, it clears. The mother can then continue to breastfeed and the jaundice does not return.

❑ During the 48 hours, the mother should express her milk. You can pasteurize it at 56°C for 15 minutes or boil it for a few seconds, and she can give it to her baby by cup; she can give the baby breastmilk from another mother; she can give artificial milk, by cup.

❑ Make sure that the mother understands that she has to express and boil her milk for *only 2 days*. Then she can breastfeed normally again.

Continue breastfeeding a baby with jaundice.

7.8 FEEDING SICK CHILDREN

Mothers sometimes stop breastfeeding when a baby is ill. When the child is well again, the milk may have dried up or the child may refuse to suckle. An important part of the care of any sick baby is to support breastfeeding to enable it to continue, and to admit the mother with the baby if he needs treatment in hospital.

− Children recover from illnesses more quickly if they are fed.

− Breastmilk is the most nutritious, easily digested food for a sick baby and it may be particularly helpful for recovery.

− Children with diarrhoea may refuse to take solids but they may breastfeed as much as when they are well. If they continue to breastfeed, they recover more quickly.

− If a baby is frightened or in pain because of the illness, breastfeeding can comfort him.

A sick child recovers more quickly if he continues to breastfeed.

How to feed a sick baby less than 6 months old

For babies less than 6 months old, breastmilk should be the only source of nourishment. The mother should avoid supplements.

If the baby is able to suckle
❏ He should continue to breastfeed as much as he can. An ill baby may suckle less strongly, or for a shorter time, than when he is well. But he may be willing to suckle more often. If the mother offers him the breast frequently, he may take as much milk as when he is well.

If the baby cannot suckle
❏ The mother can express her milk and give it to the baby by cup, or spoon, or tube. Babies with pneumonia may be too breathless to suckle; babies with other illnesses may be too weak to breastfeed. Most babies can be fed by cup or spoon. Occasionally tube feeding is necessary. Expressing breastmilk helps to keep up the mother's supply as well as nourishing the baby during the illness.

If a baby is having oral rehydration solution
❏ Give the ORS by cup in addition to breastmilk.

If the baby's nose is blocked
❏ Show the mother how to clean it (see Section 5.7).

When the baby recovers from his illness
❏ He should continue to breastfeed. His mother may need extra help and support at first if he is unwilling to suckle (see Section 5.7).
❏ Help the mother to build up her milk supply (see Section 10.5).

How to feed a sick child of 6 months or more
Breastmilk is an important food during illness for children throughout the whole of the first and second year of life.

A child who is ill and unwilling to take much solid food may be willing to breastfeed because the breast is an important source of comfort. With the comfort the child gets valuable nourishment. If he suckles more than before the illness, the breastmilk supply should increase.
❏ The child should continue to breastfeed as often as he wants.
❏ The child also needs some other food.
- Give him *small* meals of anything that he will eat, for example soft porridge. Try to give nourishing food (see Section 9.5).

- Feed him frequently—5 or 6 times a day if possible.
- As soon as he recovers, feed him extra food to make up for the lost growth (see Section 9.5).

Give a child extra food after an illness.

7.9 FOLLOWING UP A CHILD AFTER AN ILLNESS

Following children up after an illness is an important part of health care.

❏ Try to see both mother and child several times to:
- Make sure that breastfeeding continues, and to help with any problems.
- Make sure that the mother can give the child the extra food that he needs.
- Weigh the baby every week or every month and enter the weights on his growth chart.

❏ Make sure that he:
- Regains the weight he lost during the illness.
- Continues to grow.

This is an important way to prevent growth failure.

CHAPTER EIGHT

Breastfeeding and the mother

8.1 WHEN THE MOTHER IS ILL

A common reason for a mother to stop breastfeeding is because she becomes ill, for a short time or a long time. Some mothers stop for very minor illnesses such as a cold.

However, it is seldom necessary to stop breastfeeding and it is much more dangerous to start a baby on artificial feeds than it is to let him feed from his sick mother.

How the problem may arise

1. A mother believes that she cannot breastfeed if she is ill
When you treat a woman for illness, always ask her: "How old is your youngest child?" "Does he breastfeed at all?"

❏ Reassure her that she can continue to breastfeed the baby even during her illness.

If she has an infectious illness, it is much more likely to be transmitted to the baby by droplets, or on her hands, than by breastfeeding. The baby will already have been exposed while she was developing the illness. Her breastmilk probably contains antibodies, which are the best protection for the baby.

❏ If she is very unwilling to breastfeed, ask her to express her milk. Her breasts will continue to produce milk and she can breastfeed again when she is well.

Help ill mothers to continue breastfeeding

2. A mother says that her milk dried up when she was ill
Milk dries up because the baby stops suckling, not because of illness. However, if a woman has a fever and loses a lot of fluid from sweating, her milk supply may decrease.

To prevent the milk from drying up, encourage her to:
❑ Continue breastfeeding if possible.
❑ Drink plenty.
❑ Express her milk.
❑ Let the baby breastfeed again as soon as possible.

Someone can feed the baby by cup meantime, either from the mother's EBM or from artificial milk.

She may need to breastfeed more often to build up her supply when she is well again.

3. A health worker thinks that it is dangerous for an ill mother to continue to breastfeed her baby
In the past, health workers often advised women to stop breastfeeding if they were ill. If the mother had TB or leprosy, mother and baby would be separated. Now we know that it is much more dangerous for the baby to stop breastfeeding than to stay with the mother.
❑ Keep the mother and baby together.
❑ Protect the baby with BCG immunization. If necessary, treat him also for the infection.
❑ Sometimes it helps if a relative cares for the baby while the mother is still infectious. The relative takes the baby to the mother to breastfeed.

4. The mother is admitted to hospital and she leaves the baby at home
Mothers may be admitted to hospital for treatment or with another ill child. They leave the baby behind to be fed by someone else with cow's milk or thin cereal porridge. The baby may become ill because of the artificial feeds. He may refuse to breastfeed when his mother goes home after the separation, especially if he has been fed by bottle.

❑ If a mother is admitted to hospital, ask her: "How old is your youngest child?" "Does he breastfeed at all?" "Can someone bring him to you here?"
❑ Try to admit the baby with the mother so that she can continue to breastfeed.
❑ If necessary, show the family how to cup feed.

5. The mother is mentally ill

Mothers may become mentally ill for a time after childbirth (puerperal psychosis, or puerperal depression). They usually recover and look after their children normally after some months. The illness is not passed to the baby.
❑ Keep the baby with the mother if possible.
❑ Let her breastfeed the baby.
❑ Find a helper (usually a relative) who can be with her all the time to make sure that she does not neglect or injure the baby.

6. The problem affects the breast

If a woman has mastitis or a breast abscess, she may decide to stop feeding the baby—from that breast or from both breasts. It should not be necessary to stop breastfeeding.
❑ Help her to continue (see Section 5.2).

7. The mother has HIV infection

Most babies who get AIDS are infected before they are born. Very few babies get AIDS through breastmilk. The risks of bottle feeding are greater than the very small risk of getting HIV from breastfeeding.
❑ Breastfeed the baby normally.

If you admit a mother to hospital, admit her baby with her.

Building up the milk supply again

If a woman stops breastfeeding because of illness, and her milk supply decreases, help her to increase it again when she is well (see Section 10.5).

If the baby "refuses", you may need to teach him to breastfeed again (see Section 5.8).

8.2 CAESARIAN SECTION

Caesarian section should not prevent a woman from breastfeeding her baby, and it should not affect her milk supply. However, she may need extra help in the beginning.

As soon as she recovers consciousness after the operation, she can hold the baby and give him his first breastfeed. This is usually possible within 4–6 hours. A normal baby needs no food or drink before his mother can feed him. He can just wait until she is ready.

The baby can then stay in a cot beside the mother's bed and she can feed him whenever he is hungry. Mothers may need help to put the baby to the breast for the first few days. They need help to find a comfortable position in which to feed the baby, to turn over, and to move the baby from one side to the other. At first, it is often easiest to feed the baby lying down. Later, holding the baby in one of the "twins" positions may help (see Figure 28).

Whatever position the mother uses, make sure that the baby faces her and suckles in a good position.

8.3 BREASTFEEDING AND THE MOTHER'S MEDICINES

Sometimes a health worker fears to let a baby breastfeed if the mother is taking medicines, in case the drug passes into the milk and harms the baby. However, most drugs pass into the milk in very small amounts which rarely affect the baby. To stop breastfeeding is more likely to be dangerous than most medicines.

A very few drugs can be harmful
They are only prescribed in special circumstances:
– Anti-cancer drugs; anti-thyroid drugs; radioactive substances; repeated doses of ergot (one dose postpartum is not harmful).

A few drugs may cause mild side effects
Try to avoid using these drugs and prescribe an alternative if possible. However, do *not* stop breastfeeding if they are the drug of choice or the only drug available:

– Diazepam; barbiturates; tetracycline; sulphonamides; chloramphenicol.

A few drugs decrease the milk supply
Try to avoid using them:
– Oestrogens; thiazide diuretics.

Most drugs are safe
Most of the common drugs for short illnesses are safe, for example most antibiotics, antipyretics, anticoagulants and most contraceptives. Most long-term drugs are also safe, for example those for TB, leprosy, epilepsy, or for psychiatric illness.
❑ If a mother is on regular strong drugs, try to ask the advice of a doctor or pharmacist.
❑ Let the mother continue to breastfeed while you try to find out more.
❑ If you are worried, try to find an alternative drug.
❑ Watch the baby for side effects.

8.4 BREASTFEEDING AND SEXUAL INTERCOURSE

Women in some communities have heard that sexual intercourse harms their milk. However, breastmilk is not harmed in any way by sexual intercourse. The only danger is that of another pregnancy.
❑ If you feel that a woman is worried about this, you may need to mention it yourself. She may be unwilling to ask.

8.5 BREASTFEEDING AND CHILD SPACING

Breastfeeding can delay the return of ovulation and menstruation (see Section 2.3), so it is an important way to delay a new pregnancy. The effect depends on the baby suckling frequently, and continuing to feed at night, to stimulate the secretion of prolactin and other hormones. As soon as the baby starts supplements of any kind, he suckles less. The mother is likely to ovulate and menstruate again.

In many countries, breastfeeding contributes very much to the spacing of births. For some mothers, it may be the only family planning method available. Health workers and mothers need accurate information about the reliability of the method and about how to ensure the maximum effect.

In most women, menstruation returns before conception. But a few women ovulate and can conceive before they start to menstruate again.
- Before the baby is 6 months old, less than 2% of mothers who breastfeed fully are likely to conceive before they menstruate.
- After the baby is 6 months old, 10–15% of women may conceive before they menstruate.

Family planning is also important to help breastfeeding to continue. A pregnancy too soon may change the milk and deplete the mother.

The Lactational Amenorrhoea Method of family planning, or LAM

If a woman wishes to use breastfeeding for child spacing she must breastfeed fully as follows:

❑ Breastfeed exclusively or almost exclusively for the first 6 months (see Section 3.7).
❑ Breastfeed frequently, with no long intervals. She should breastfeed whenever the baby wants to:
- Both night and day.
- Eight to ten times or more in 24 hours.
- With no interval longer than 6 hours between feeds.

She must understand that LAM will only be effective before her periods return, and before she gives the baby supplements. If she has a period, or if she gives the baby regular supplements, she must use another method of family planning. This is both to prevent pregnancy and to allow her to continue breastfeeding.

For protection after 6 months, she should:

❑ Continue frequent breastfeeding for 2 years or more. After 6 months, the baby needs other foods as well as breastmilk and the risk of pregnancy increases. However, she still has some protection against a new pregnancy if:
- She continues to breastfeed frequently both night and day.
- She breastfeeds before each feed of supplements.
- Her menstruation has not returned.

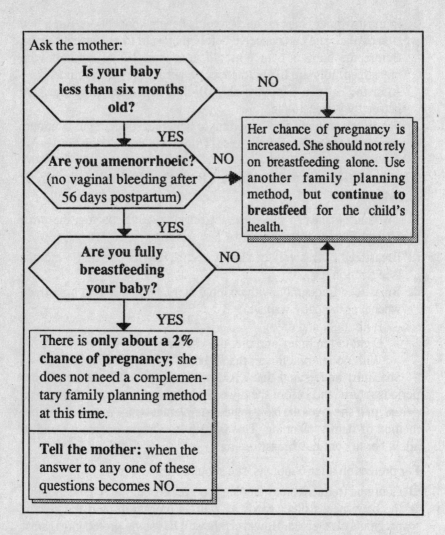

Figure 31. Use of the Lactational Amenorrhoea Method (LAM) for child spacing during the first 6 months postpartum.

(from Labbok, M. *et al.* 1990. *Guidelines for Breastfeeding in Family Planning and Child Survival Programs*. Institute for Reproductive Health, Georgetown, Washington, D.C.)

What to do

When you care for mothers postnatally:

❏ Talk to each mother about her next pregnancy and about how she can delay it until she is ready for another baby. Help her to choose the best method of family planning for her.

❏ Explain that:
  – Her babies will be healthier if they are born 3 years or more apart.
  – She will be stronger if she does not become pregnant until 6 months after she stops breastfeeding. Her body needs this time to recover.

❏ Explain about how breastfeeding can help to prevent a pregnancy, as well as being good for the baby's health.

❏ She should plan to use another method of family planning immediately if:
  – Her baby is 6 months old.
  – She begins to menstruate.
  – She starts to give the baby other food or drink.

❏ If a woman does not want to rely on breastfeeding for family planning, she should start another method *within the first 6 weeks after delivery*— that is, no later than her final postnatal check.

Other methods of family planning include:

Oral contraceptives

Combined pills which contain oestrogen as well as progesterone may reduce the amount of breastmilk that a mother produces. It is best to avoid them during lactation if possible.

However, if the baby is already receiving supplements, and if no other method of family planning is available, it is better for both mother and child to use combined pills than to risk an early pregnancy.

Progestagen pills which contain only progesterone do *not* decrease breastmilk flow and they may even increase it. They are suitable for use during lactation and they are effective.

Injectable contraceptives

Depo-Provera does not decrease the breastmilk supply and it may increase it, so this contraceptive can be used during lactation.

Physical methods of contraception

Intrauterine device (IUD)

An IUD does not affect lactation in any way and is very suitable for use in breastfeeding mothers. Insertion needs to be immediately postpartum, or delayed until 6 weeks after delivery. Between those times, the IUD is more likely to be expelled. Check regularly during breastfeeding that the IUD is still in place.

Condoms, spermicide creams and foams, and diaphragms

These methods are all suitable for use during lactation if they are acceptable to the couple. They are effective, but only if used correctly. Condoms also help to prevent HIV infection.

Other methods of natural family planning

Periodic abstinence, the calendar rhythm method, the ovulation method based on symptoms, or the temperature method, can all be difficult to use during breastfeeding, especially before menstruation has returned. They may demand long periods of sexual abstinence. With proper counselling, however, they may be appropriate for some couples.

8.6 BREASTFEEDING AND A NEW PREGNANCY

Medically it is quite safe to continue to breastfeed during a new pregnancy if the mother can eat adequately. Some mothers continue to breastfeed the older baby throughout the new pregnancy and sometimes they breastfeed both babies together after the new one is born. This can be helpful if the second pregnancy comes very quickly, and when the first child is too young to stop breastfeeding.

However, most mothers prefer to stop. Some believe that it is harmful to one or both babies to continue to breastfeed. They may be so afraid that they stop breastfeeding the older child very quickly.

Some mothers find that their breasts become tender with the new pregnancy. The hormonal changes may decrease the supply of breastmilk and may make it more salty. During the last few weeks of pregnancy, the breasts begin to produce colostrum again.

What to do

Discuss with the mother that:
❑ Breastfeeding during pregnancy is not harmful to either of the babies.
❑ If she stops breastfeeding the older child, she should do it slowly (see Section 9.6). Stopping suddenly can be harmful and can make the older child ill.
❑ She must eat enough herself, because she is now feeding three people.

8.7 BREASTFEEDING AND MENSTRUATION

Some mothers believe that it is dangerous to breastfeed during a menstrual period. Some women feel some breast tenderness.

In some women, the taste of breastmilk changes at this time. Sometimes a baby becomes unwilling to suckle, or he refuses, and the mother may think that there is something wrong with the milk. However, the quality of the milk remains the same and it cannot make the baby ill.
❑ Reassure women that it is completely safe to continue breastfeeding during a period.

Some women worry if their periods do not return soon after their baby is born.
❑ Reassure them that it is normal not to have a period for a year or more when they are breastfeeding.

CHAPTER NINE

Supplements and weaning

9.1 BREASTMILK AFTER 6 MONTHS OF AGE

Breastmilk is normally all that a baby needs until about 6 months of age. Some time around that age, he outgrows the milk supply. The amount of breastmilk that the mother can produce does not decrease, but it is no longer enough by itself. The baby needs other food as well.

Breastmilk continues to be the main source of food for several more months. During the second year of life, breastmilk can provide one-third or more of the energy and nutrients that a child needs. It can be difficult for a small child to eat enough of the other foods to grow and stay healthy on them alone.

9.2 WHEN TO START OTHER FOOD

There is no exact, fixed time for a baby to start taking other foods. All babies are different and all mothers are different. Most mothers have enough breastmilk for their babies for 6 months. Some have enough for 9–10 months. But some babies begin to outgrow their mother's milk at about 4–5 months. The average age that a baby needs to start other foods is about 6 months. The earliest they should be given is 4 months.

Start solid foods when a baby is about 6 months old.

How to decide if a baby is getting enough food

Weigh the baby regularly (see Section 6.2). Plot the weights on a growth chart and find out if he is growing.

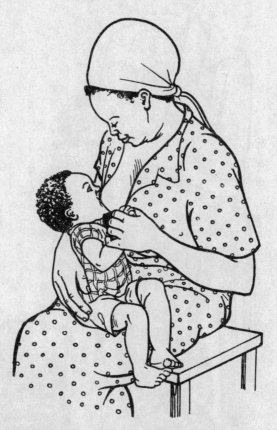

Figure 32. Breastfeeding an older child.

If he is gaining weight
If his growth line rises and follows the reference curve, then he is growing so he is getting enough food.

If he is not gaining weight
If his growth line is flat and does not follow the reference curve, he is not growing so he needs more food.

Figure 33. At about 6 months of age, babies start to reach out for their mother's food.

If he is below 4 months of age
❑ Try to increase the mother's breastmilk supply (see Section 10.5).

If he is 4 months or more
❑ Try to increase the mother's breastmilk supply.
❑ Consider starting other food as well.

Many babies stop growing at about 6 months of age when they outgrow the milk supply. They may appear quite healthy for several months, but their growth line becomes flat (see Figure 34). The flat growth line shows that breastmilk by itself is no longer enough for the baby.

Other ways in which babies become ready for food

At about 6 months of age, babies show that they are ready for food in other ways. They can sit up, they reach out for things that they see and they put them into their mouths. If a mother holds her baby on her lap while she is eating, the baby reaches out for her food (see Figure 33).

Before 6 months, babies may push solid food out of their mouths with their tongues. After 6 months, they become able to take solid food into their mouths more easily. They start to get teeth and to chew.

At about 6 months, also, a baby's stomach becomes ready for adult food. A newborn baby does not have all the enzymes necessary to digest foods other than milk. For example, his intestines contain only small amounts of amylase, to digest starch. By about 5–6 months of age, a baby can digest most food.

9.3 STARTING FOOD AND WATER TOO EARLY

It is dangerous to start any food or drink before the baby is 4 months old. The food or water may be contaminated so that the baby may get diarrhoea.

The baby may suckle less at the breast so he gets less milk; and the mother is more likely to conceive again.

Give only breastmilk until a baby is at least 4 months old.

Water and glucose water

Thirst

Some mothers, and some health workers, like to give babies drinks of plain water or glucose water. This is not necessary—breastmilk contains all the water that a normal baby needs, even in a very hot climate. Even drinks of plain water make a baby take less breastmilk, so that his growth slows down.

❑ Explain to a mother that if her baby seems thirsty, he should suckle at the breast. He will get the water that he needs and some nourishment also. Suckling will keep up the supply of breastmilk.

Soft stools

Some mothers think that they should give water to very young babies to make the stools soft and easy to pass.

❑ Reassure them that a breastfed baby always has soft stools (see Section 3.5) and water does not make them softer (unless it gives the baby diarrhoea).

Babies who may need extra water

- Artificially fed babies may need extra water because there is too much salt in cow's milk.
- Babies with diarrhoea need oral rehydration solution while they have diarrhoea.

❑ When the diarrhoea stops, stop the extra fluids or they may interfere with breastfeeding.

Fruit juice

Breastfed babies do not need fruit juice. Breastmilk contains enough vitamin C for a baby until he is 6 months old. Artificially fed babies may need fruit juice.

Cow's milk and formula supplements

A mother may give cow's milk or formula supplements because the baby cries; because the baby wants to suckle a lot; because she believes that the baby needs more than breastmilk alone; because she has to be away from the baby, for example to work. Often the supplement is left all day in a bottle for someone else to give to the baby.

The dangers of milk supplements
- The baby is more likely to have diarrhoea and vomiting. The diarrhoea may become persistent.
- The baby is more likely to have respiratory infections such as pneumonia and ear infections.
- The baby may suckle less at the breast, or may refuse to breastfeed, especially if the feeds are given by bottle.
- Breastfeeding may stop and the breastmilk may dry up.
- If the baby gets too little milk, he may stop gaining weight and become undernourished.
- If he has too much milk, he may become unhealthy from overweight. He may have all the problems of being overweight in later childhood.
- If the milk overloads his stomach and intestine, he may get diarrhoea and vomiting.
- The baby is more likely to have allergies such as asthma and eczema.

How to advise a mother about supplements
- ❑ Explain the dangers of supplements and advise her not to give them.
- ❑ Explain that the cause of crying or of the need to suckle may not be hunger (see Sections 2.9 and 6.4). Discuss the other reasons why a baby may cry and suggest other ways to comfort the baby.
- ❑ Discuss how she can avoid giving cow's milk or formula if she goes out to work (see Section 6.5).
- ❑ Explain about feeding babies from cups instead of bottles (see Section 10.4).

Cereals, teas and other foods

Some mothers start to give cereal porridge or other starchy food at about 1 month of age, sometimes by bottle.

Some mothers give babies bottle feeds of tea, sodas or other drinks.

Cereals can make a baby *lose* weight because:
- Cereal porridge may look thicker than milk but it is more dilute and contains less nutrients, especially less fat.

- A small baby cannot digest the starch well.
- The porridge fills the baby's stomach and he suckles less at the breast.
- Mothers often make the porridge a long time before the baby eats it. Bacteria grow in the food and cause diarrhoea.

Teas and other drinks contain little nourishment except some sugar. But they fill the baby's stomach so that he suckles less at the breast.

❏ Talk to mothers about the value of giving *only breastmilk* until the baby is at least 4 months old.

❏ If a mother has to give a supplement before the baby is 4 months old, she should give milk and not cereal. She should give it by cup and not by bottle.

❏ Health workers should set an example and not give solids to their babies before they are 4 months old.

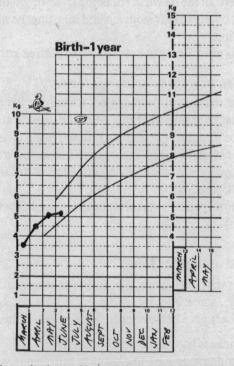

Figure 34. Growth chart showing growth faltering at 2–3 months of age because supplements were introduced too early.

Early supplements can result in:
Diarrhoea.
Insufficient breastmilk.
Early pregnancy.

9.4 STARTING OTHER FOOD TOO LATE

The custom in some places is not to give a child any other food until he is over 1 year old. This is too late and may cause malnutrition.

Children who do not start to eat other foods at about 6 months of age stop growing. Some babies continue to grow on breastmilk alone until they are 9–10 months old, but most babies outgrow their mother's milk supply some time between 4 and 8 months.

If a child does not start to eat other food at about 6 months of age, it may be more difficult to teach him to eat solid food.

Between 5 and 9 months of age, most babies are very hungry. They are willing to eat more solid food and to try new tastes. But after 9–10 months of age, they become more fussy. They do not want to try new things. So if a mother waits until her baby is 9–10 months old before she gives him food she may find that it is difficult to teach him to eat solids.

What to advise mothers
❏ Start to give other food when the baby is about 6 months old. Some babies need to start at 4 or 5 months.
❏ Give a little very soft food, such as porridge, at first, until the baby gets used to eating it.
❏ Gradually increase the amount of food and the different kinds of food.

Starting other food late can cause malnutrition.

9.5 WHAT FOODS TO GIVE

The first food that a baby eats should be soft. Most mothers give a cereal porridge. It is not necessary to buy packaged baby cereals. These are expensive, and no better than home-made porridge. Their only advantage may be convenience.

By about 9 months, a baby can eat most of the family foods if they are cut up and made easy to eat.

Staple, or main foods, such as cereals (maize, millet, rice, wheat) and root crops (cassava, potatoes) are all starchy. One of the problems of starchy foods is that they are "bulky" or big. Cereals are bulky because they are cooked with a lot of water. Root crops are bulky because they grow with a lot of water in them. A child's stomach is small. He cannot easily eat enough of a bulky, starchy, staple food to get all the energy (or calories) that his body needs.

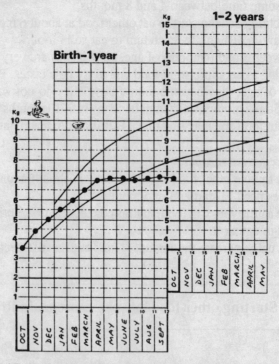

Figure 35. Growth chart showing growth failure after 6 months of age because weaning foods were started too late.

Figure 36. Feeding a child soft porridge by cup and spoon.

To give a child all the nourishment that he needs, his family needs to:

❏ Feed him often—about five times a day.

One of the reasons why children do not eat enough is because they do not eat *often* enough. Many mothers are out working all day and they only have time to feed the child once or twice a day.

It is not necessary to cook five times a day—some of the meals can be nourishing, cold snacks.

❏ Add some energy-rich food to the bulky staple.

Oil, margarine (such as Blue Band), cooking fat, and groundnuts are all rich in energy. One spoonful of one of these foods added each day to a child's porridge may provide all the extra energy that he needs.

115

Frying food in fat or oil also increases the energy content. *Mandazis* make a good snack because they are fried.

Sugar is another energy-rich food that can be added, but too much sugar causes tooth decay.

❏ Add some protein-rich food to the staple.

Beans, groundnuts, milk and eggs are rich in protein.

❏ Add some green or coloured vegetables or fruit.

These provide the extra vitamins that a child needs after he is 6 months old.

❏ Give the child his own plate of food. Small children eat slowly and they may not get enough when they share a plate with other members of the family.

9.6 STOPPING BREASTFEEDING

There is no need to stop breastfeeding if the child wants to continue, even after 3 years. But some children stop by themselves some time after they are 1 year old.

Breastmilk is an important source of nourishment throughout the second year, especially for families who find it difficult to get enough nutritious food for children. Breastmilk also continues to protect children against infection. If mothers stop breastfeeding early, the child may stop growing or lose weight. This is an important cause of malnutrition.

Encourage mothers to continue breastfeeding until the child is at least 2 years old. Mothers often need a lot of support to continue when they are pregnant, when they have to work away from home, when they are ill or the child is ill, or when they seem not to have enough breastmilk. Try to give them the support that they need and look for other groups in the community who can also help (see Section 12.3).

If a mother decides to stop breastfeeding, she should do it slowly. Stopping suddenly may make a child unhappy so that he refuses to eat other food and becomes ill and malnourished.

To stop breastfeeding slowly, a mother should:

❏ Make sure that the child is eating enough other food. Increase the number of meals that the child has.

❏ Increase the length of time between breastfeeds, so that the number decreases by about one feed a day each week or two for 2–3 months.

❑ At first she might stop giving breastfeeds during the morning; after a week or two she might also stop breastfeeding during the afternoon. For that part of the day, she can avoid situations which make the child think of breastfeeding, such as having the child on her lap when she sits down to eat. If the child is old enough to understand, she may be able to explain that he can breastfeed later, but that now is not the time.

❑ Give the child breastfeeds at other times.

❑ Stop the night breastfeeds last.

❑ Give the child loving attention and make him feel close to his mother in other ways.

❑ She should not push the child away if he insists on breastfeeding.

Small children need to eat five times a day.

CHAPTER TEN

Techniques and appliances

All mothers should learn to express their breastmilk. They can start to learn during pregnancy and they can practise soon after birth.

Expressing milk is useful to:
- Feed a low birth weight or sick baby.
- Relieve engorgement.
- Keep up the milk supply when the mother is ill.
- Relieve leaking breasts.
- Leave milk for the baby when the mother goes out or goes to work.

10.1 EXPRESSING BREASTMILK BY HAND

Hand expression is the most useful method. It needs no appliance, so a woman can do it anywhere, at any time. It is easy to hand express when the breasts are soft. Sometimes it may be more difficult when the breasts are very engorged and tender.

A woman should express her own milk. The breasts are easily hurt if another person tries. If you are helping a woman to learn how to express, show her on your own body as much as possible. If you touch her, be very gentle.

Stimulating the oxytocin reflex

A mother can only express her milk effectively if her oxytocin reflex works, so that the milk flows. When the breasts are very engorged, it is difficult for the oxytocin to reach the muscle cells to make them contract. You need to be able to help the mother to get her reflex to work.

Let the mother:
- ❏ Find somewhere quiet and private, or with a supportive friend. Some mothers can express easily in a group of other mothers who are also expressing for their babies.
- ❏ Hold the baby, with skin-to-skin contact if possible. The mother can hold the baby on her lap while she expresses, or she can look at the baby, or at a photograph of the baby.
- ❏ Take a warm soothing drink (but not coffee).
- ❏ Warm the breast. Apply a warm compress or warm water, or have a warm shower.
- ❏ Massage the breasts gently towards the nipples. Some women find that it helps if they stroke the nipple and areola gently with finger tips or with a comb, or if they gently roll the closed fist over the breast.
- ❏ Ask a helper to rub her back. The mother sits down, leans forward, folds her arms on a table in front of her and rests her head on her arms. Her breasts hang loose. The helper rubs the knuckles of her fist firmly up and down the mother's back. She should rub either side of the spine, from the neck to the shoulder blades, for 1–2 minutes.

Preparing a container for the expressed breastmilk (EBM)

Explain how the mother should:
- ❏ Choose a cup, glass, jug or jar with a wide mouth.
- ❏ Wash the cup in soap and water, and leave it in the sun to dry. (She can do this the day before.)
- ❏ Pour boiling water into the cup, and leave it for a few minutes. The sun and boiling water will kill most of the germs.
- ❏ When she is ready to express her milk, she pours the water out of the cup.

How to express the milk

Explain how she should:
- ❏ Wash her hands thoroughly.
- ❏ Sit or stand comfortably, and hold the cup near the breast.
- ❏ Put her thumb on the areola *above* the nipple, and her first finger on the areola *below* the nipple, opposite the thumb.
- ❏ Press the thumb and finger inwards towards the chest wall.

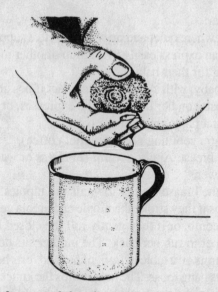

(a) Place the finger and thumb on the areola and press inwards towards the chest wall.

(b) Press the areola behind the nipple between the finger and thumb.
Figure 37. How to express breastmilk.

❑ Now press the areola behind the nipple between the finger and thumb. She must press behind the nipple, so that she presses on the lactiferous sinuses beneath the areola.

❑ Press and release, press and release.
This should not hurt—if it hurts, the technique is wrong. At first no milk may come, but after she has pressed a few times, milk starts to drip out. It may flow in streams if the ejection reflex is active.

❑ Press the areola in the same way from the *sides* to make sure that milk is expressed from all segments of the breast.

❑ Express one breast for at least 3–5 minutes until the flow slows, then express the other side, and then repeat both sides again. She can use either hand for either breast, and change when they tire.

❑ She should not slide her fingers along the skin. She should not squeeze the nipple itself. Pressing or pulling the nipple cannot express the milk. It is the same as the baby sucking only the nipple (see Section 2.7).

To express milk adequately takes 20–30 minutes, especially in the first few days when only a little milk may be produced. It is important not to try to express in a shorter time.

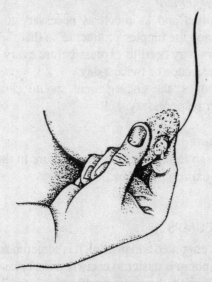

(c) Press from the sides to take milk from the other segments.
Figure 37. How to express breastmilk.

Every woman should learn to express her milk.

How often and how long to express breastmilk

To feed a LBW or sick baby
❑ A mother needs to express as much milk as she can, every time the baby needs to feed—usually every 3 hours, or 8 times in 24 hours (see Section 7.2).

If she expresses more milk than her baby needs, she can give it to another baby whose mother cannot express enough, or to a LBW baby whose own mother's milk has not yet come in (see Section 7.3).

To keep up the supply of breastmilk when the mother is ill
❑ Express as much milk as possible as often as the baby would normally feed.
❑ Feed it to the baby if possible.

To relieve engorgement
❑ Express as often and as much as necessary to keep the breasts comfortable and the nipples protractile so that the baby can suckle. Some mothers may need to express before every feed. Others only need to express once or twice a day.

After some days, the engorgement should clear and expression should no longer be necessary.

To relieve leaking
❑ Express enough milk to reduce the pressure in the breasts. It is not necessary to express very much milk.

10.2 BREAST PUMPS

If the breasts are engorged and painful, it is sometimes helpful to express with a pump. A pump is easier to use when the breasts are full. It is not so easy to use when the breasts are soft.

It is important to stimulate the mother's oxytocin reflex in the same way as for hand expression.

Figure 38 shows a hand pump which is available in many chemist shops. It is sometimes called a "breast reliever".

How to use a hand breast pump

This pump is a special glass tube with a rubber bulb at one end. The other end of the tube is wide to fit over the nipple. Show the mother how to:

❏ Compress the rubber bulb to push out the air.
❏ Place the wide end of the tube over the nipple.
❏ Make sure that the glass touches the skin all around, to make an airtight seal.
❏ Release the bulb. The nipple and areola are sucked into the glass.
❏ Compress and release the bulb again, several times. After compressing and releasing a few times, milk starts to flow. The milk collects in the swelling on the side of the tube. Break the seal to empty out the milk, and start again.

Cleaning and sterilizing the hand pump

It is important to clean and sterilize a pump every time it is used. Hand pumps are difficult to clean properly. Milk may collect in the bulb and it is difficult to clean out. The milk which collects is often contaminated so hand pumps are not suitable for collecting milk to feed to a baby. They are useful mainly to relieve engorgement when hand expression is difficult.

Electric pumps

Electric pumps are more efficient and are suitable for use in hospitals. However, all breast pumps can easily carry infection. This is especially dangerous if more than one woman is using the same pump.

It is important for women to learn to express their milk by hand, and not to think that a pump is necessary.

Sterilize a breast pump every time you use it.

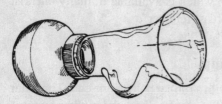

(a) A hand breast pump.

(b) A mother expressing milk with a hand breast pump.
Figure 38. Expressing milk with a hand breast pump.

10.3 THE "WARM BOTTLE" METHOD

This is a useful technique to relieve engorgement, especially when the breast is very tender and the nipple is tight, and hand expression is difficult. Explain to the mother how she can:

❑ Find a large bottle (for example 1 litre, 700 ml, or 3 litres), if possible with a wide neck (3 cm diameter). Clean it thoroughly.

❑ Ask the family to heat some water. Pour a little of the hot water into the bottle to start warming it, then almost fill the bottle with hot water. Let it stand for a few minutes to warm the glass. (The heat should also kill any germs in the bottle.)

❑ Wrap the bottle in some cloth and pour the hot water back into the pan.

❑ *Cool the neck of the bottle* and put it over the nipple, touching the skin all around to make an airtight seal.

(a) Putting hot water into a bottle.

(b) Pouring it out.

Figure 39. Preparing a hot bottle

❑ Hold the bottle steady. After a few minutes the bottle cools and makes a gentle suction which pulls the nipple into the neck of the bottle.

❑ The warmth helps the oxytocin reflex, milk starts to flow and collects in the bottle.

❑ When the flow of milk slows, release the suction and take the bottle off. Do not leave it on too long or it may hurt the nipple.

❑ Pour out the milk, then do the same for the other breast.
Sometimes when the woman first feels the suction, she is surprised and pulls away. So you have to put more hot water in the bottle and start again.

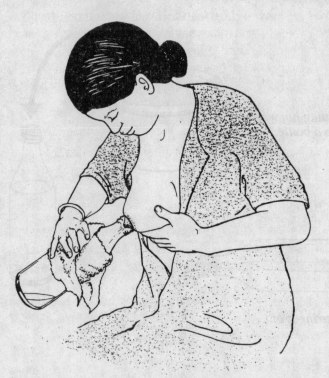

Figure 40. A mother putting a hot bottle over her nipple.

❑ After some time, the acute pain in the breasts becomes less and hand expression or suckling may become possible.

10.4 FEEDING A BABY BY CUP

Cups are much safer than bottles. Feeding bottles should not be necessary. Never use feeding bottles in a hospital. They suggest to mothers who attend that bottle feeding is safe.

Cups have these advantages

– They are easy to clean with soap and water if boiling is not possible.
– They are less likely than bottles to be carried around for a long time, giving bacteria time to breed.
– They cannot be left beside the baby for the baby to feed himself. The person who feeds a baby by cup has to hold the baby and give him some of the contact that he needs.
– They do not interfere with suckling at the breast.

You can feed even small LBW babies from a cup as soon as they can swallow (see Section 7.2). Cup feeding is less tiring for a LBW baby than bottle feeding.

Spoon feeding

Spoon feeding is quite safe but it takes longer and you need three hands.

Some mothers give up spoon feeding before the baby has had enough. Mothers are more likely to continue with cup feeding. So cup feeding is better for most babies.

If a baby is very ill, for example with difficult breathing, it may be better to feed the baby with a spoon.

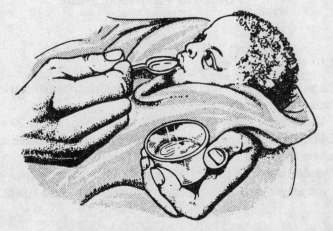

Figure 41a. Spoon feeding a baby.

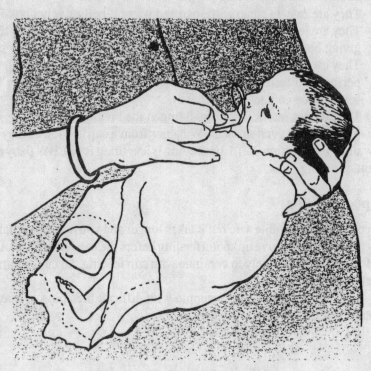

Figure 41b. Cup feeding a baby.

How to cup feed a baby

❑ Use an ordinary cup—not one with a spout which is difficult to clean. Use a small cup if possible.
❑ Hold the baby closely, sitting a little upright (see Figures 29 and 41).
❑ Hold the small cup or glass to the baby's lips. He may make suckling movements. Pour in a little milk at a time, very slowly.
❑ Give the baby time to swallow. Let him rest between sips.
❑ If you are worried about giving too much, try using a spoon.

10.5 INCREASING THE SUPPLY OF BREASTMILK

If a woman's breastmilk supply is poor it will increase *if the baby suckles often to stimulate the breasts*.

If she has stopped breastfeeding, and her milk has dried up, suckling can make the milk flow again. This is called *relactation*.

If the baby is still breastfeeding, the milk supply increases in a few days. If he has stopped breastfeeding, it may take 1–2 weeks or more before much milk comes. It is easier if the baby is still young and if he stopped breastfeeding recently. But it can be done at any time, even in a woman who has not breastfed for years and who wishes to feed a grandchild. Even a woman who has never breastfed can produce milk if she suckles an adopted child.

Try to help the mother and baby at home if possible. Occasionally it may be helpful to admit them to hospital for a week or two so that you can give her enough help—especially if she may use a bottle again at home.

How to increase the breastmilk supply

❑ Discuss the problem which may have caused a poor breastmilk supply, and sort it out if you can. For example, if she has started to give the baby bottlefeeds, advise her to stop them.

❑ Try to give the mother confidence that she can produce breastmilk again or increase her supply.

  Try to talk to her twice a day if possible.

❑ Make sure that she has enough to eat and drink.

  Eating more may not increase a woman's milk supply. But if she is undernourished, she needs to build up her strength and energy.

  If she is not undernourished, food and warm nourishing drinks may help her to feel confident.

  If you know of a locally valued lactogogue (see below), advise her to take that.

❑ Encourage her to rest more, and to try to relax when she feeds the baby.

❑ She should keep the baby near her and do as much as possible for him herself.

❑ The most important thing is to let the baby suckle more—at least 10 times in 24 hours.

- She can offer the breast every two hours.
- She should let him suckle whenever he seems interested.
- Sometimes it is easiest to get the baby to suckle when he is sleepy.
- She should keep him with her and breastfeed at night.
- She should let him suckle longer than before at each breast.

❏ Make sure that the baby suckles in a good position.

❏ Try not to give the baby other milk feeds, especially if he is less than 6 months old, and if the mother is still producing breastmilk. However, if her breastmilk has dried up, other milk feeds may be necessary, while waiting for breastmilk to come back.

❏ She should give the other feeds from a cup, not from a bottle. She should not use a "dummy".

❏ If the baby refuses to suckle on an "empty" breast, show her how to drip milk down the nipple as the baby suckles, or help her to use a nursing supplementer (see Section 10.6).

❏ To start with, give the baby the full amount of artificial feed for a baby of his weight (150 ml per kilo per day), or the same amount that he has been having before.
Each day, reduce the total by 30 – 50 ml.

❏ Check the baby's weight and urine output, to make sure that he is getting enough milk.

❏ In a few cases, a senior health worker may prescribe the mother a drug for a short time (see below).

To increase the milk supply, let the baby suckle more often.

Drinking fluids

Many mothers notice that they are more thirsty than usual when they are breastfeeding, especially near the time of a feed. They should drink to satisfy their thirst. However, taking more fluid than they feel they need does not increase their milk supply. It might even reduce it.

Lactogogues

Lactogogues are special foods, drinks, or herbs which people believe can increase a woman's milk supply. In parts of Kenya, women drink *wimbi* porridge, made from millet and sorghum flour, to help them lactate well. Some women like the porridge soured. Other people find that warm soup or milk are helpful.

Probably lactogogues do really help. They do not work like drugs, but they work psychologically—because they increase the woman's confidence and help her to relax. Also, they may help her nutrition.

Some women notice that a small amount of an alcoholic drink makes their milk flow—perhaps because it reduces their anxiety. This cannot be recommended as treatment, however, because alcohol can also interfere with lactation.

Drugs to increase the milk supply

There are two drugs that may help to increase the milk supply. If you are sure that a woman does not have enough milk, and if you have tried all the other ways to increase her milk supply, then a senior health worker may be prepared to try one of these drugs. However, they are unlikely to work unless the baby is suckling in a good position and is breastfeeding frequently.

Chlorpromazine: Give 25 mg three times a day for 1 week. If necessary, repeat the course once more.

Metoclopramide: Give 10–15 mg three times a day for up to 3 months.

10.6 NURSING SUPPLEMENTER

A nursing supplementer can help a mother to build up her milk supply. A hungry baby may suckle at an "empty" breast a few times, but he may become frustrated and refuse to suckle any more, especially if he has become used to sucking from a bottle. A nursing supplementer can help to overcome this problem.

How to use a nursing supplementer

A nursing supplementer is a fine tube which acts like a drinking straw. The tube passes from a cup of milk to the baby's mouth (see Figure 42). The milk can be diluted cow's milk or formula, or EBM if available.

❑ Put the end of the tube along the mother's nipple, so that the baby suckles the breast and the tube at the same time. He gets milk from the cup through the tube. His suckling stimulates the nipple, which starts the production of breastmilk.

❑ Use a very fine infant feeding tube or other polythene tubing.

❑ If you do not have a very fine tube, use a wider one. However, if the tube is too wide, the baby gets the milk from the cup too easily, and he does not suckle hard enough to stimulate the nipple. Put a paper clip on the tube or show the mother how to pinch the tube with her fingers to control the flow, or she can tie a knot in the tube.

❑ Clean and sterilize the tube of the supplementer and the cup each time you use them.

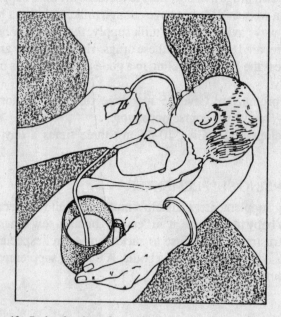

Figure 42. Baby feeding from the breast and using a nursing supplementer.

Dripping milk on to the breast

Mothers sometimes find their own way to give a baby milk while he suckles. One way is to drip milk on to the breast above the nipple, so that it runs into the baby's mouth as he suckles. Figure 43 shows a mother dripping milk from a cup. You can also drip milk from a syringe or dropper if one is available.

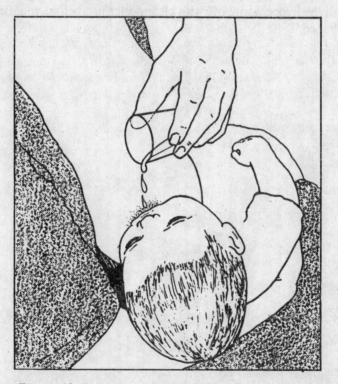

Figure 43. Dripping milk on to the breast for the baby.

10.7 CLEANING AND STERILIZING THE APPLIANCES

Clean and sterilize breast pumps, bottles and nursing supplementers each time you use them. This is important to prevent both infection in the baby and infection of the breast.

How to sterilize the appliances

Either:

❏ Boil them for at least 20 minutes in water.

Or:

❏ Soak them between feeds in diluted hypochlorite (bleach)* in a covered container or pan.

❏ Add 1 spoonful of hypochlorite to 1 litre of water.

❏ Wash the hypochlorite off with clean water just before you use the appliance.

---

* Household bleach in a 0.5% solution is quite safe for sterilizing the appliances. With many brands this is made by adding 2 spoonfuls (20 ml) bleach to 1 litre of water. Check the strength of your local brand.

CHAPTER ELEVEN

Counselling

The early chapters of this book give you the technical information that you need to help mothers to breastfeed. This chapter explains how to plan your work and how to counsel individual mothers.

You cannot do everything that we suggest here for every mother. As you gain experience, you will learn to decide what sort of help different women need, and which women need extra help.

Figure 44. Looking at the woman as a whole helps you to decide who needs extra help.

11.1 THE IMPORTANCE OF PERSONAL SUPPORT

Personal contact and support really helps breastfeeding to succeed. This may be from health workers, counsellors, family members, or from other breastfeeding mothers in the community. Radio broadcasts, newspaper articles and lectures can increase people's knowledge, but they may not change what mothers do. Person-to-person help is necessary to convince mothers to put the ideas into practice.

Support for a breastfeeding mother means a kind person who can:
- See her often, help with practical tasks, and avoid saying anything critical.
- Reassure her that she can breastfeed and that her milk is perfect and sufficient.
- Praise her for what she is doing right.
- Explain what is normal.
- Advise her if she does not know what to do.
- Help her if she has a problem.
- Encourage her to persist.

The wellbeing of the woman

Before you discuss with a mother how she feeds her baby, think of the woman herself, and her difficulties and problems.

The success of breastfeeding depends more than anything else on the mother's own wellbeing, and on how she feels about herself and her life situation.

❏ Think about her working situation. Does she have to travel far? Work difficult hours? Can she eat at work?

❏ Think about who she has to help her—relatives, neighbours, husband, maid, friends.

❏ Think about her self-confidence. How is she coping with herself and her personal problems?

❏ Think about her attitude to this baby or this pregnancy. Did she really want it?

Successful breastfeeding depends on the wellbeing of the mother.

Sometimes you can help a woman to sort things out. Sometimes you can help her to find someone who lives nearby to help her. Many mothers will have problems that you can do nothing about.

But if you take an interest, and show sympathy, you can make her feel better and that alone may help her.

11.2 ANTENATAL PREPARATION

Every health worker who sees women antenatally should feel responsible for these things:
- Preparing the woman psychologically for breastfeeding.
- Discussing with the woman how to look after herself.

Psychological preparation

Talking to groups

There are some general things that all women need to understand. It may be easier to talk to them in a group and to encourage group discussion and questions. These include:

❏ The advantages of breastfeeding, the benefits of colostrum, and the dangers of artificial feeding.

 Make it clear which you think is best, but do not make women feel anxious and guilty. Do not let them think that you are forcing them, or that you will blame them for doing something else. Try to let mothers feel that they can choose, but help them to *want* to breastfeed.

❏ How breastfeeding works and what they are likely to experience, especially in the first few days.

 For example, they need to know about how milk comes in, and that the baby needs to suckle to help the milk flow, even if the breasts seem "empty".

❏ If you have changed the practices in hospital—for example if you have stopped giving prelacteal feeds, or if mothers now keep their babies with them after delivery—mothers need to know or they may be unwilling to accept the new practice.

137

❑ How to express milk.

Explain why it is useful to know how to express milk. Demonstrate the technique and encourage them to practise the movements.

Some women believe that they should express the colostrum that the breasts secrete in the last few weeks of pregnancy. It is not necessary to express colostrum, but it is not harmful.

Talking to individual women

It is also important to talk to each woman individually at some time during pregnancy. During the last 3 months may be the best time. Talk to her more than once if you can. Record on her antenatal card that you have talked to her about breastfeeding.

❑ Ask her if she has thought about feeding her baby.

Show that you are interested in her personally, and help her to tell you about any doubts and fears that she might have. Be kind and gentle, and listen to what she says sympathetically.

❑ Ask about her previous experience of breastfeeding.

If she has had a bad experience before, for example a breast infection, explain how she can prevent that problem and succeed better this time.

If a previous baby died, and she or her relatives blame the death on her milk, she may need extra counselling and help.

❑ Encourage her to believe that she *can* breastfeed.

Explain that all women can breastfeed if they want to. Reassure her that if she has any difficulty, you and your colleagues will be pleased to help her to overcome the problem.

❑ Encourage her to ask questions. Make sure that she understands the advantages of breastfeeding, and what she will experience. If she knows what to expect, she will feel more confident and her milk will flow better.

❑ Make sure that she has someone experienced who has breastfed to support her at home. If not, try to find someone who can help, or make a note to try to see her more often yourself.

❑ Examine her breasts and check the nipples for protractility. If the nipples protract well, reassure her that her breasts are very good for breastfeeding.

If the nipples do not protract well, or if they are inverted, reassure her that she can breastfeed. Explain how the nipples will improve when the baby starts to suckle. You can give her any extra help that she needs to get started (see Section 5.4).

❏ You may want to explain that it is not necessary to stretch or toughen the nipples to prepare them during pregnancy—it probably does not help. (You may prefer to say nothing.)

A checklist of antenatal advice

These are the things that it is useful for a mother to know before she delivers.

1. Her breastmilk is always the best food for her baby. The quality of the milk will always be good whatever her diet.
2. The size and shape of the breasts does not matter. Small breasts and large breasts both produce perfect milk in sufficient quantity, and a baby can suckle from any of them.
3. Breastfeeding need not spoil her figure. It should help her to lose weight after the baby is born. Having a baby always alters the breasts—whether or not the mother breastfeeds. Most changes that you see in older women are partly due to age. If she wears a well-fitting brassiere or other support while she breastfeeds, her breasts will return to a good shape when she stops.
4. Bottle feeding is dangerous. If family and friends urge the use of a bottle, she can explain that this practice is no longer recommended because it causes much illness.
5. Let the baby suckle soon after delivery—within an hour if he is willing. She should keep the baby with her and let him suckle whenever he wants to from the first day. This helps the mother's milk to come in.
6. She can make one or two of her dresses open at the front so that the baby can reach the breast easily. This helps her to breastfeed modestly, without exposing the breasts.
7. All mothers feel more emotional and sensitive than usual for a few weeks after delivery. It helps to know that these feelings are normal and that they will pass.

Looking after herself

It may be very difficult for a woman to make any change in her way of life. But discuss with her that it is important to keep her own body strong.

If she can rest a little more, or get someone to help her, it may benefit both her and her baby.

If possible she should eat more green vegetables and protein-rich foods such as beans. These foods help to keep her strong and prevent anaemia.

Women who are thin also need to eat more energy foods.

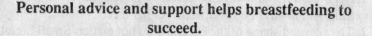

Personal advice and support helps breastfeeding to succeed.

Figure 45. A health worker counselling a breastfeeding mother.

11.3 AFTER DELIVERY

Health workers in maternity wards have a great responsibility. They must:

❑ Give the baby to the mother immediately after delivery.

❑ Make sure that the baby stays close to the mother and that breastfeeding is unrestricted.

❑ Make sure that the baby does not have any prelacteal feeds.

❑ Build the mother's confidence and help her with her breastfeeding technique.

For the first hour or two, leave the mother alone to cuddle and to love the baby, to bond with him, and to put him to the breast as soon as he is willing.

Next time the baby breastfeeds, watch her, and see how she is managing.

Observing an early breastfeed

❑ Be calm and gentle. Try not to hurry, try not to be noisy and do not talk too much.

❑ Congratulate the mother on her baby and tell her that she is doing well. Remember that your most important job is to encourage the mother and to give her confidence.

❑ Ask the mother how she feels she is doing and if she has questions or worries. Try to answer them and to reassure her.

❑ Be very careful not to say anything critical, or even anything doubtful. Remember that a mother is more sensitive than usual and may easily lose confidence in herself and her milk.

Check the following points

❑ Look at the mother's general appearance and expression.

Does she look happy or miserable? Is she looking at the baby and bonding with him, or is she turning away and ignoring him? If she is miserable or ignoring the baby, she may have a problem with her life situation, and with bonding. She may need extra help and counselling.

❑ Make sure that she is in a relaxed position.

It does not matter if she is sitting down or lying down, but it must be a relaxed position.

❑ Make sure that the baby takes enough of the breast into his mouth and suckles in a good position (see Section 2.8). If the suckling position is poor, help the mother to improve it. Make sure that she understands what is needed so that she can do it herself.

A checklist of postpartum advice

These are the points that it is useful to check through with mothers soon after delivery:

1. The breasts may not feel very full at first. This does *not* mean that she does not have any milk. They are producing colostrum now, and the mature milk will "come in" in a few days.
2. Colostrum is exactly what a baby needs for the first few days. She should not throw it away.
3. Frequent suckling helps the milk to come in and it is the best way to build up her milk supply.
4. When the milk "comes in", the breasts may be very full and a little swollen for a few days. This is common and it will pass. Breastfeeding should prevent them becoming too swollen.
5. The baby does not need feeds of cow's milk, glucose, or water, or anything else.
6. The length of a feed does not matter. Some babies are slow feeders, some are fast feeders. Let the baby suckle until he releases the breast by himself.
7. She should let the baby finish the first breast before she offers him the second. Then he gets plenty of hindmilk. He may only want a little from the second breast, or none at all. She can start on the other breast next time, so that both make plenty of milk.
8. Breastfeeding helps to stop the bleeding. The mother may feel quite painful contractions (in the uterus) and a rush of blood during early breastfeeds. That is normal and it is a good sign that her milk will flow well.
9. Suckling at night helps to keep up the milk supply. It is safe for the baby to sleep in the same bed as his parents so long as they have not taken drugs, or drunk too much alcohol.
10. It is not necessary to wash the breasts before every feed. She should not use soap on the nipples.

Choose a convenient time to show her how to express her milk.

11.4 THE FOLLOWING WEEKS

Many problems with breastfeeding can arise in the first 2 weeks.

If a mother delivers at home

The midwife, traditional birth attendant, or relative who helped with the delivery, usually continues to look after the mother. They can support the mother and give her advice whenever she needs it. Usually they help breastfeeding, but some practices may cause problems.

If a mother delivers in hospital .

She may be discharged 48 hours before lactation is established. There may be nobody nearby who can help or support her.

Her first appointment at the hospital may be the 6 week postpartum check. It may be difficult for her to leave the house before that time.

The best thing is for a community nurse or midwife or counsellor to visit each new mother as soon as she goes home—but that is not possible yet in many places.

The first 2 weeks at home are a danger time for breastfeeding.

Preparing a breastfeeding mother to leave hospital

❑ Give her a growth chart for the baby. Fill in the date of birth, the birth weight, and any reasons for special care. Explain what the chart is for, and ask her to bring it with her any time she brings the baby to see a health worker.

❑ Explain when her follow-up appointment is and ask her if she has any questions.

❑ Encourage her to go on breastfeeding and reassure her that she can do it.

❑ Remind her that the baby does not need any other food or drinks for about 6 months.

❑ Explain that she should breastfeed whenever the baby wants to. She does not have to follow any hospital routines at home. If breastfeeding is unrestricted, the baby will not cry so much.

❑ Discuss again that "more suckling makes more milk". If she thinks that she does not have enough milk, breastfeeding the baby more often for a few days should build up her supply. Breastfeeding at night is especially valuable.

❑ Discuss how she must look after herself, rest, and eat a good diet.

❑ If you can see her husband, discuss with him how he can help his wife.

❑ Advise her what to do if she needs help or advice with breastfeeding.

- If there is a community nurse or midwife, she may be able to ask them for help.
- She can return to the ward or go to the clinic at any time before the date of her follow-up appointment.
- If there is a mother-to-mother support group nearby, she can contact them. In Nairobi, for example, she can contact the Breastfeeding Information Group (BIG) for help (P.O. Box 59436, Nairobi. Tel: 749 899).

The postnatal appointment at the MCH clinic

Remember to check about breastfeeding.

❑ Ask her how breastfeeding is going, and if she has any questions. If she seems to have problems, let her tell you about them.

❑ Check her breasts. You may notice healthy fullness, dripping of milk, normal nipples. You will also see if there is engorgement, nipple fissure, or another abnormality.

❑ Notice if her clothing permits easy breastfeeding and if she has brought along the baby. Has she a bottle in her bag?

❑ Notice if she holds the baby close and looks pleased with him, or if she looks worried or depressed.

❑ Watch the baby breastfeeding and make sure that he suckles in a good position. Ask her if suckling is comfortable for her.

❑ Weigh the baby and enter his weight on his growth chart. Make sure that he has regained his birth weight and that his growth line is following the reference curve (see Section 4.9).

❑ If both mother and baby are doing well, praise her. Explain what the growth chart shows. Reassure her that the baby is getting plenty of breastmilk. Encourage her to give the baby nothing else until he is at least 4 months old.

(a) A breastfeeding mother holding the baby close and looking at him.
Figure 46. Notice how the mother holds the baby.

❑ If there seems to be a problem, discuss it with her, and try to help her. Many problems are very minor, and reassurance or simple advice is all that is needed (see Section 11.6).
❑ If she has to return to work soon, explain how she can continue to breastfeed at the same time (see Section 6.6). Make sure that she knows how to express her milk and how to feed the baby with a cup.
❑ Ask her if she needs any help with family planning. Explain the LAM method (see Section 8.5).

A checklist of postnatal advice (at 2 weeks)

Two weeks after the birth, gently explain to the mother that:
1. She should continue with unrestricted frequent breastfeeding, by day and by night. This is the best way to keep up a good milk supply and to delay a new pregnancy.
2. She should not give supplements before the baby is at least 4 months old, and if possible not until he is 6 months old. Supplements can cause diarrhoea and interfere with breastfeeding. Her breastmilk might decrease and she would be more likely to become pregnant.

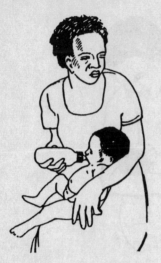 

(b) *A bottle feeding mother holding a baby loosely on her knee and looking bored with him.*

(c) *A breastfeeding mother holding her baby loosely like a bottle feeding mother, and looking depressed. This baby may not be getting enough milk.*

Figure 46. Notice how the mother holds the baby.

3. Her breasts may soon feel soft again. This does *not* mean that she has "lost" her milk.

4. It is common for a baby to cry some of the time. Crying does not mean that she does not have enough milk. She does not need to give a supplement. She can hold the baby more and let him suckle more often (see Section 6.4).

5. If she does not breastfeed the baby often, for example if she is away from him, or if she is too busy to feed him, her breasts will make less milk. She cannot "save up" milk for the next breastfeed.

6. If at any time she thinks that she does not have enough milk, she should let the baby suckle more often for a few days. Her milk will increase.

7. Some breastfed babies do not pass a stool for several days. This does not mean that the baby is constipated. Some breastfed babies pass 8 or more very soft stools a day. It does not mean that the baby has diarrhoea. No treatment is needed.

11.5 GENERAL ADVICE IN THE CLINIC

Remember that everything that you do in an MCH clinic or outpatient department can influence breastfeeding.

Provide drinking water for breastfeeding mothers

When they arrive in the clinic, they may be thirsty. Give the mothers a drink and ask them to feed their babies.

Take down all formula advertisements

Destroy them, or send them to someone who is responsible for the Code (see Section 12.6).

Make sure that you do not have any posters or calendars in your clinic which advertise formula or bottles of any kind. Throw away any empty formula tins that are used as pencil holders, door stops or plant pots, etc. Put up posters of breastfeeding instead.

When you weigh a baby

Check on how he is feeding. Write "breastfeeding" on the growth chart. Show approval to mothers who are breastfeeding and encourage them to continue—including during the second year.

It may be helpful to discuss some of the points in the "checklist of postnatal advice".

If a baby's growth slows down in the first 4 months, help her to build up her breastmilk supply and advise against supplements.

When you immunize a baby

Remind the mother that breastfeeding also protects her baby against infection. Encourage her to put the baby to the breast if he cries after the injection.

When you treat a sick baby

Discuss with the mother how she can continue to breastfeed. Tell her that breastmilk is the best food for a sick child. If the baby is crying, ask the mother to put the baby to the breast to comfort him.

If the baby cannot suckle, teach the mother how to express her milk and feed it by cup.

When you treat a sick mother

Discuss with her how she can continue to breastfeed.

When you give family planning advice

Explain how breastfeeding can help to space pregnancies (see Section 8.5) and how delaying the next pregnancy helps breastfeeding.

When you give health education talks

Make sure that breastfeeding and weaning are topics included in the talks at MCH clinics—whether in hospital outpatient departments, in health centres, or at outreach clinics. You do not have to talk about breastfeeding every week. It should be just one of the topics in a health education plan which includes family planning, immunization, diarrhoea and other health matters.

Try to make your talk a discussion with the mothers, not a lecture. Let them ask questions and try to answer them. Listen to their experiences and try to understand the reasons that they give for what they do.

Try to have something to show the mothers to start the discussion for example a photograph, or a dirty feeding bottle. You may prefer to do a short role play with another health worker, or with one or two of the mothers, to start the discussion.

When you discuss nutrition

Remember breastfeeding. Write "BREASTMILK" on your nutrition posters. Remember to talk about it as an important source of every nutrient through the second year of a child's life. Remember that stopping breastfeeding early helps to cause undernutrition.

If you give out DSM, make it clear that this is to add to food for children over 6 months of age. Mothers should never put DSM into a drink or a bottle feed for a baby.

Everything in the MCH clinic may influence breastfeeding.

11.6 THE MOTHER WITH A PROBLEM

Most problems are small and easy to solve, so it is sad if they lead to breastfeeding failure. Some women understand their own problems clearly. Other women have no idea at all what is wrong, or they have a completely mistaken idea—for example that their milk is "too thin", or that it is bad. Sometimes the main problem is that the mother is worried about not having enough milk—she lacks confidence.

To help mothers, a health worker must have a good knowledge of lactation, and experience of working with breastfeeding mothers. If she has breastfed her own baby, that is an advantage, but it is not essential.

The counselling approach

It is important to understand the difference between *advising* and *counselling*.

When you advise a person who is ill:
- You decide the best treatment.
- You tell the patient what to do.
- You want the patient to have confidence in you.

When you counsel a breastfeeding mother:
- You help her to decide what to do.
- You give her new skills so that she can succeed.
- You want her to have confidence in herself.

Health workers who are used to treating ill people sometimes need to alter their approach to counsel breastfeeding mothers. (It is often easier for a woman who is not a health worker to counsel mothers.)

Sometimes we are so keen to help that we give advice too quickly, without really understanding the situation. But this is not always helpful. Mothers need support, and telling them only what they are doing wrong is not very supportive. If you also praise a mother for what she is doing right, then it is easier to encourage her and to give her confidence.

Caring for a woman with a breastfeeding problem

Here we discuss the general approach to the management of a woman with *any* breastfeeding problem.

Specific problems are discussed in earlier sections.

You need the same organized approach that is necessary for most health problems.

1. Take a history from the woman.
2. Examine her and the baby.
3. Try to make a diagnosis—or at least form an impression of the cause of the problem.
4. Sometimes you can recommend treatment.
5. Occasionally you need to refer a woman for more specialized help.
6. Often you can help with her breastfeeding technique.
7. Usually you can explain and suggest something helpful.
8. Always you can listen, sympathize and reassure.

Taking a history

To take a good history, you need to talk with the mother in a gentle, sensitive way and *listen carefully* to what she says.

❑ Greet the woman in a kind and friendly way.

❑ Encourage her to tell you as much as possible in her own way. This is the best way to learn about her. Listen, then answer in a way which shows that you understand—for example say: "Yes, it is worrying when a baby cries"; do not say: "Oh, that is nothing to worry about, all babies cry." Encourage her to say more, for example with: "How do you feel about that?" or "Mmm, Aha".

❑ Look at the child's growth chart and see what it tells you.

❑ You will need to ask some questions. But try not to ask too many; and be careful not to ask things which the mother or the growth chart has told you already.
   - Try to ask questions that she has to give you a complete answer to. Try not to put the answer into the question so that she only says "yes" or "no". That does not help you or her. For example, do not ask: "Did you breastfeed your last child?" She may have given the child both breast and bottle feeds, but the answer "yes" does not tell you that. It is better to ask: "How did you feed your last child?" and "What else did he need?"
   - Avoid using words which sound judging, for example "right","wrong", "badly", "well", "enough", "good", "properly". Say: "How is the baby sleeping?" and not "Does he sleep well?"

Say: "How is your breastmilk supply?" and not "Do you have enough milk?"

You usually need to learn about these straight-forward things
- The woman herself, her age, her work, her family situation.
- Her previous children, how she fed them, any problems.
- This baby: any problems during pregnancy, or with delivery.
- When he was born; how much he weighed.
- Where he was born.
- When she first held the baby and put him to the breast.
- Where the baby stayed during the first few days.
- How long it took for her milk to come in.
- The condition of her nipples and breasts since delivery.
- What sensation she has when she tries to feed (signs of ejection reflex).
- What feeding pattern she has followed (frequency and length of feeds).
- Whether she gives any supplementary feeds and if so, what and why.
- How the baby behaves about feeding and sleeping.
- How much time she spends away from the baby each day.

You may need to ask about more difficult things which can help you to learn whether the woman really wants to breastfeed.
- What have people told her about breastfeeding?
- Would she like to be able to leave the baby with someone else?
- Does she have to follow any special rules?
- What does her husband say? What does her mother say?
- Did she want this pregnancy at this time?
- Is she happy about having the baby now?

These are all difficult things to ask about and she may not want to talk about them at first. Wait, and ask again later, or on another day. Perhaps you need to find somewhere more private to talk to her.

Always check the baby's weight and fill in his growth chart.

Examination of baby, breast and suckling position

The order in which you do the examination varies depending on the behaviour of the baby. If he is suckling when you first meet the mother, greet her quietly, ask her to continue and just sit and watch the breastfeed. You can take the history and examine her breasts later on. If the baby is asleep, talk to the mother until he wakes up. Sometimes you have to go back later to observe a breastfeed.

❑ Look at the baby's growth chart, weigh him if necessary and decide if he is growing well.

❑ Look for signs of illness or abnormality in the baby.

❑ Ask the mother if you may examine her breasts. Explain what you are going to do and touch her very gently.

– Are the breasts soft, or full, or engorged? (See Section 5.1.)

– Are her nipples long, average, short, or inverted? Are they protractile? (See Section 5.4.)

– Are there any fissures or white spots on her nipples? (See Section 5.3.)

– If the woman has an active ejection reflex, milk may flow when you examine her nipples. That is a helpful sign. But touching her may also stop the reflex. If no milk flows, it tells you nothing, so say nothing about it.

❑ Ask the mother if you may watch her breastfeed the baby. Let her sit somewhere quiet and private if possible. You should also sit comfortably nearby. Do not stand over her. Ask her to put the baby to the breast in her usual way.

Look at the mother

– Does she sit in a comfortable relaxed position or does she seem uncomfortable and tense?

– Does she seem happy with the baby and does she look at his face?

– Does she hold him close, support his bottom and touch him a lot? Or does she hold him away from her and shake him on her knee?

– Does she offer the baby the whole breast or does she pinch the nipple and try to push it into the baby's mouth?

Look at the baby

– Is he relaxed and calm, or is he tense and fussing at the breast?

- Does he seem to be trying to find the breast (rooting or "homing-in" when young, reaching for the breast when older) or does he seem to refuse?
- Is his whole body facing his mother's body or does he have to turn his head to reach the breast?
- Look at his suckling position. A poor position may not be so obvious as in Figure 6. He may have only a few signs.

How does the breastfeed finish?
- How long does the baby suckle for?
- Does he release the breast himself or does his mother take him off?
- Does he appear full and satisfied?
- Does the nipple look squashed as it comes out of his mouth?

Explanation and advice

When the problem seems clear to you, explain to the mother what you think the difficulty may be and discuss what she could try to do.

❏ Be careful not to sound critical of what she has done. It makes a lot of difference to say: "It might help to feed him more often" instead of "You are not feeding him often enough"; or: "I think he isn't taking quite enough breast into his mouth" instead of "You are not putting him on to your breast in the right way".

❏ Be supportive and encouraging.
- Look for things that she is doing right and praise her for them. For example, that she breastfeeds often; that she feeds the baby at night; that she is trying to breastfeed at all.
- Try to build up her confidence. Reassure her that she can succeed, that her difficulties are not unusual and most women find that they can overcome them.

Try to tell her a story of another woman's success. Collect your own good stories from the women whom you help.

❏ Help her with her breastfeeding technique.
- If she has engorgement, help her to relieve it.
- If the problem is the baby's suckling position, help her to improve it.

153

Sometimes overcoming a problem of technique and getting the baby to suckle well relieves her other worries.

❑ Counselling about the feeding pattern
Do not tell her what to do. Instead, give her the necessary information, and then suggest what she could try. For example, "Bottle feeds can make a baby unwilling to suckle. Do you think that you could stop the bottle feeds?" or "If a baby suckles more often, it increases the milk supply. Could you breastfeed more often?" Discuss with her a plan for the next few days. Let her decide what to do for herself as much as possible.

❑ Counselling when the mother is not enthusiastic about breastfeeding
 – Try to share your enthusiasm with her. Help her to feel good about breastfeeding so that she really wants to try.
 – If she has other worries and difficulties, it is often better to talk about them, and to leave breastfeeding for another time. Do not make her feel that you are trying to force her to breastfeed, or that you will blame her if she does not.

❑ Encourage her to ask you questions about anything she is not sure of, or that she is worried about.

Make sure that you see the woman and her baby again soon.

Follow up

Make sure that you see the woman again in a few days. Visit her at home if you can. If you cannot visit her, encourage her to come back to the health centre or clinic. If there is a breastfeeding support group nearby, introduce her to them, and see if it is possible for them to help her.

Weigh the baby regularly and follow her progress when she comes for other visits—for immunization or for treatment.

CHAPTER TWELVE

Promoting breastfeeding in the community

12.1 THE COMMUNITY'S ATTITUDE TO BREASTFEEDING

Whether mothers breastfeed successfully or not depends partly on the attitude of other people in the community—fathers, grandmothers, relatives, friends, employers, community leaders and others.

Where people think that breastfeeding is normal, most mothers succeed. In these places it is important to protect breastfeeding and to make sure that people understand how valuable it is, so that it continues.

Where people think of breastfeeding as old fashioned, difficult, embarrassing, or a nuisance, mothers are more likely to fail. In these places it is necessary to promote breastfeeding and to encourage people to value it more, so that more mothers succeed.

What you do depends on where you live and work, for example on whether you are in a rural area or a city. It also depends on your own particular skills.

Learning about the local situation

First you must know what the attitudes and practices in your community are. You do not need to do a survey. Talk to people, and ask in a humble way, and you can learn what you need to know.

Ask mothers about how they feed their babies, and their reasons for what they do. Ask other family members, including fathers and grandparents, what they think about breastfeeding.

Ask other people in the community, such as adolescents, people who employ women workers, religious leaders and shopkeepers (especially if they sell formula and feeding bottles).

Talk to your colleagues; talk to health and community workers. Make sure that you know what the practices are in local hospitals, in the maternity wards, in women's and children's wards, and in outpatient departments.

Learn as much as you can about how many mothers have unsafe feeding practices:
- How many never start to breastfeed.
- How many mothers give prelacteal feeds.
- How many mothers start to give bottle feeds or other supplements before 4–6 months.
- How many stop breastfeeding before the child is 2 years old.
  Try to understand their reasons for what they do.

Try to decide:
- Which women are most likely to adopt unsafe practices (for example, young women, or single women).
- Who influences their decisions about infant feeding (for example, their friends, or grandmothers).

Attitudes and ideas which affect breastfeeding

Decide which attitudes and ideas help breastfeeding so that you can encourage them. For example:
- Breastfeeding is healthier.
- Babies should breastfeed when they want to.
- Babies should sleep with their mothers.
- Breastfeeding should continue for 2 years or more.

Decide which attitudes and ideas lead to unsafe practices in your area, so that you can discourage them. For example:
- Colostrum is not good for a baby.
- Babies should not suckle until the milk "comes in".
- A woman should stop breastfeeding if she becomes pregnant.
- If a baby is sick, he should stop breastfeeding.
- Breastmilk may go bad if the baby does not suckle for a day.

- Many babies need more than breastmilk, especially if they cry.
- Mothers often do not have enough breastmilk.
- Bottle feeds make a baby fatter and healthier.
- Bottle feeding is more fashionable.
- Breastfeeding may spoil a woman's figure and interfere with her relationship with men.
- It is better to be free to go out with friends.
- Working mothers can't breastfeed and work.
- It is embarrassing to breastfeed in public.

Planning what to do

When you understand why mothers stop breastfeeding early and why they use bottles, you can think of ways to encourage them to breastfeed. For example:
- How could you make breastfeeding more fashionable?
- Who could give mothers more confidence in their breastmilk?
- How could you reach mothers sooner with better family planning advice?
- Who could help working mothers to breastfeed?

You need to decide:
- What facts you most need to communicate (for example, that feeding bottles are dangerous, and are not necessary).
- Whom you need to communicate them to (for example, young men and women).
- How to communicate them (for example, by discussions, or through drama).
- Who is the best person or group to help make messages effective? (Perhaps young members of community groups.)

12.2 MAKING HEALTH SERVICES MORE SUPPORTIVE

Many women fail to breastfeed because health services do not support them. In many places the most urgent need is to make sure that health service practices support breastfeeding: in maternity wards, other hospital wards, in outpatient departments, in MCH and family planning clinics, in community health.

Not all health workers understand about breastfeeding. Some may be very negative about it, especially if their own children were bottle fed. Help them to understand that you do not criticize or blame them. They did what seemed best for their babies at the time. But explain that new knowledge is available and we should help mothers differently now. Try to find some colleagues who think that breastfeeding is important, and you may be able to help each other to get things changed.

Try to make sure that your colleagues in other departments have up-to-date information. Explain what you are trying to do and ask them to give mothers the same messages that you give. Your colleagues may not be as interested in breastfeeding as you are. But they may be pleased to send mothers who need help to you.

Working with traditional birth attendants

In some areas traditional birth attendants (TBAs) have an important influence. Their practices may be helpful or harmful.

Helpful practices include putting babies to the breast soon after delivery and encouraging unrestricted feeding. TBAs sometimes blame younger mothers for keeping their babies waiting.

Some TBAs know how breastfeeding immediately after delivery can help to deliver the placenta and stop uterine bleeding. They know how continuing to breastfeed helps to delay a new pregnancy. They give mothers confidence and practical help, and feed them warm nourishing drinks such as *wimbi* porridge, or bone soup, to help the milk to flow. Some TBAs know how to express milk to treat breast engorgement and they understand that if the baby breastfeeds more often, the supply of milk increases. Some TBAs know that for the baby to get the milk, the mother must hold him close to her breast.

Harmful practices in some areas include not giving colostrum, and not putting the baby to the breast until the milk "comes in". Some TBAs advise supplements for a baby who cries, even if the baby is very young. Some may taste a mother's milk when the baby is ill, and say that it is too salty or too sweet, and that the baby should not feed from the breast.

Try to talk to the TBAs in your area; show them respect and ask them about their practices. Explain what you have learnt about breastfeeding, for example about the value of colostrum, or the dangers of early supplements. Praise them for those practices which help breastfeeding.

Ask if they would be able to change the more harmful practices.

If there is a TBA training programme in your area, make sure that their training includes breastfeeding.

12.3 WOMEN'S GROUPS

Women's groups are very important for breastfeeding. Ask if you can talk to groups in your area. Ask them about local practices and about why women do what they do. Explain why you think breastfeeding is important and discuss the sorts of help that women may need.

Be ready to talk to women who bottle fed their children. They may find it hard to believe that breastfeeding is better. Encourage them to talk about why they decided to bottle feed and show respect for their reasons. Do not make them feel that you blame them. They did the best that they knew for their babies. Their children may be very healthy and that is good. However, new knowledge is available and it is important to protect other children from risk.

Encourage groups to make breastfeeding one of their activities. Ask if they would be interested in forming a breastfeeding promotion group to help educate the community and to support breastfeeding mothers. Some of them may wish to become breastfeeding counsellors.

Help groups to decide what their activities will be. Some possibilities that they might consider are:
- Visiting pregnant and newly delivered mothers in the neighbourhood to encourage them to breastfeed. They can help with practical tasks and common breastfeeding problems; they can make sure that mothers with complicated problems get more specialized advice.
- Getting groups of mothers together to discuss breastfeeding and child care.
- Talking to working mothers about how they could continue breastfeeding.
- Talking to employers about making it possible for workers with babies to breastfeed.
- Helping mothers to find ways to breastfeed modestly in public places, so that they do not feel a need to take a feeding bottle when they go out.
- Discussing the importance of breastfeeding with other members of the community, including men and young people.

159

A neighbourhood counsellor can be very good at providing continuing support, for example, to:
– Mothers who deliver in hospital and who have no-one to help them at home.
– Mothers of LBW babies, twins, and handicapped babies.
– Mothers with inverted nipples.
– Mothers who are ill.
– Mothers who need to increase their milk supply.

These mothers may need visits once or twice every day for a time and health workers are not usually able to visit so often.

In some countries, counsellors visit mothers in the maternity hospital. They help mothers both in the hospital and after they go home. Counsellors and health workers get to know each other so that they can work together to help mothers.

Women who wish to form a group, or to become counsellors, must be willing to learn about breastfeeding. They must be able to give families accurate information and to correct misinformation. They need to learn from someone with up-to-date knowledge and skills, such as a trained counsellor or a health worker who has been trained in breastfeeding. They could have a short training course or weekly training sessions. The trainer helps the group to get suitable books (such as this one) and leaflets and other materials to study. She helps them to plan their activities and continues to give support and additional training as necessary.

12.4 DIRECT MOTHER-TO-MOTHER SUPPORT GROUPS

If there are several breastfeeding mothers in a neighbourhood, they may be interested in forming a group to support each other. These "direct mother-to-mother groups", or MSGs, may be the most effective way to help mothers to continue breastfeeding after the first few weeks. They are probably more effective than health workers.

Mothers in the group (and their babies) meet regularly about every 1–4 weeks, sometimes in the home of one of the mothers. One or more of the mothers needs to be a "leader" who is accurately informed about breastfeeding.

The main activity at a meeting is to share experiences: how they feel; the pleasures of breastfeeding; the difficulties they have had and how they learnt to cope with them. They can see what they are all doing right, they can pass on skills to each other, and they can feel proud together.

At each meeting, the group may have a topic to discuss, such as "The advantages of breastfeeding", or "Overcoming difficulties". The leader does not give a lecture or do much talking. She may say a few words to introduce the topic. Then she encourages the others to talk about their own experiences and thoughts. She needs to be able to correct misinformation and to suggest solutions to problems. This helps the group to be positive and not just to complain.

The meetings provide:
– Social contact for otherwise isolated mothers.
– A source of support which builds women's confidence about breastfeeding and reduces their worry.

Meetings are a way to learn:
– How to breastfeed easily and comfortably, for example getting the baby's suckling position right.
– Useful practical ideas, such as how to breastfeed at night, or how to breastfeed modestly in a public place.
– More scientific information about how their bodies work, and about children's growth and development.

Members also help each other outside meetings. They may visit each other when they have a problem or when they don't know what to do, or when they are worried or depressed. In some places it is possible for women to support each other by telephone. They may also help mothers who are not members of the group but who ask for help.

Groups need to educate themselves about breastfeeding. They need up-to-date materials, such as books and leaflets, which they can take home to read between meetings. So they need to be in contact with some source of further information and advice.

To develop their skills, and to expand, groups need training. Suitably skilled health workers can help. But groups also need to be in contact with a more experienced mother-to-mother support group. If no national group exists, they could write for help to IBFAN Africa, P. O. Box 781, Mbabane, Swaziland; or to one of the international organizations, such as La Leche League International, P.O. Box 1209, Franklin Park, IL 60131–8209, U.S.A.).

12.5 REACHING OTHER SECTIONS OF THE COMMUNITY

It is also important to educate men, grandparents, employers, children and adolescents about breastfeeding.

Discuss with people in the local community what you are trying to do. Find out if there are groups such as village health committees or religious groups whom you can talk to.

Ask if you can come to some of their meetings to discuss your work. Listen to their views and try to decide what it is most useful to talk about with them. Encourage their helpful attitudes, as well as discussing their unhelpful ones.

Ask them if they would be willing to promote breastfeeding, and suggest ways in which they might help.

Men

Try to talk to men about the importance of breastfeeding and the dangers of bottle feeding. Discuss how they can help their wives to breastfeed. Try to point out how it benefits them if their wives breastfeed, for example, it saves money, and their children will be ill less often.

Explain that it does not help to buy a new mother a feeding bottle and a tin of formula, even if it is meant as a kind gift.

Employers

Talk to employers of women workers about the importance of breastfeeding. Try to discuss how they could help their employees to breastfeed if they gave 3–4 months paid maternity leave, nursing breaks, flexible working hours, and facilities to express breastmilk; or if they could provide day care centres for babies. Point out that women who have healthy babies worry about them less and this may make them better employees.

Figure 47. Some children bottle feed their younger brothers or sisters.

School children

Some children, especially in towns, see mothers bottle feeding and they may bottle feed their own younger brothers and sisters. They may grow up with the idea that that is the normal way to feed a baby. Girls may decide how they are going to feed a baby long before they have one. If they do not see that breastfeeding is natural and easy, they are not likely to decide to feed their own babies that way. By the time a baby is born, it may be too late. So it is important to start teaching children about breastfeeding before they grow up.

School textbooks sometimes talk about bottle feeding as normal. One textbook in Kenya contains the following riddle: "We have a visitor at our house. He came last night and he drinks milk from a bottle." The answer is: "A new baby." (*Msingi wa Kiswahili*, Longman, Kenya, 1982.)

❑ Encourage teachers to introduce breastfeeding into health education or sex education for both boys and girls in schools.

❑ Ask if you can give a talk to the school children in your area.

❑ Ask the children how they would like to feed their own babies, and why they want to feed them that way. Try to learn their concerns so that you talk about what interests them. This is different from what a group of parents might worry about.

❑ Try to correct any misinformation, for example that formula is better than breastmilk. They need to know why breastfeeding is important and why bottle feeding is dangerous. But these facts may not be what influences them at this age.
❑ Try to make breastfeeding appear attractive, pleasurable and modern.
❑ Encourage boys to admire women who breastfeed.
❑ Explain that breastfeeding need not change a girl's figure more than having a baby changes it.
❑ Point out that breastfeeding is much less trouble than bottle feeding and a sick baby. It need not stop a mother going out or visiting friends. It is easier to take a baby with her if she is breastfeeding.
❑ Encourage girls not to have a baby before they are ready to accept the demands that a baby makes on its mother.

Children's comic papers can help with health education. The November 1984 issue of *Rainbow* published the results of a Health and Nutrition Essay competition for children in Uganda and Kenya. Several of the winning entries mentioned that breastfeeding is good.

The CHILD-to-child Programme is developing an Activity Sheet for children, to help them learn about breastfeeding. Figures 44 and 47 are from the Activity Sheet. CHILD-to-child is becoming an important education programme for children.

For adolescents, try to show posters showing glamorous women breastfeeding. Try to get a popular singer, or a sports personality, to support breastfeeding publicly.

Figure 48. A cartoon from Rainbow *Magazine by Hezbob Enonda (14), Changiam Primary School, Kericho, published by Rainbow/ Mazingira Health Special 1984.*

12.6 MEDIA AND MATERIALS

Use the media

To reach a wider public, you need to work through the media. Whenever you can, try to use newspapers, television and radio to explain your message. This is easiest if you live in a large city like Nairobi. Newspapers are often short of material for their features page and they are glad if you give them something to write about.

For example, they may write a feature for the Woman's Page about breastfeeding, or about weaning foods, or about the Code (see Section 12.7). You might write a letter to the newspaper and hope that they will publish it.

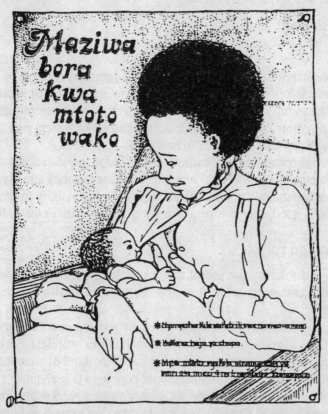

Figure 49. A good breastfeeding poster for your clinic.

Pamphlets and posters

Try to get as much interesting teaching material as you can find. The Breastfeeding Information Group (BIG) in Nairobi produces posters and information leaflets about infant feeding. These are free on request from BIG, P. O. Box 59436, Nairobi, telephone 749 899.

If you work in a hospital or health centre, make sure that you have a good breastfeeding poster up. Make sure that there are no posters that advertise any infant formula or other baby foods. If you talk to a group, try to leave pamphlets behind for the audience to read afterwards to help them to remember the message correctly.

If you have no printed posters or pamphlets, try to make your own teaching aid. Write your main message on a large sheet of paper, or draw a picture, and put it up where people can see it.

Songs

If people in the community like to sing songs, get them to make up a song about breastfeeding. Women's groups or mothers' groups sometimes enjoy making up songs. They may sing these at their own meetings. They may use a song to introduce the idea of breastfeeding at meetings of other groups, or at MCH clinics, or in hospitals.

If you know a group of children who like to sing and dance, ask them to sing a breastfeeding song. They can use a tune that they already know, and make up their own words. This may be a good activity in school. If the song is good, they can sing it to parents or even over the radio.

Drama and roleplay

Drama and roleplay are useful to get people to discuss breastfeeding, both for community education and for training health workers and counsellors.

Prepared drama can be used to start discussions in public meetings, in meetings of community groups, or in schools or hospitals. Encourage the group who will do the drama to think of the kind of situations that occur in the community, that they want people to talk about.

For example, a group could act a story about a baby who was given formula in hospital, and who never learned to breastfeed, and who then became ill with diarrhoea. One person could be a health worker who did not know how to help, or who recommended formula. Or the family at home might object to the new baby crying and insist that the mother gives bottle feeds. Or the mother might have to go back to work, so she decided to give up breastfeeding completely. Someone could act the employer complaining about mothers with babies who always get sick. There could be two babies in the play—one breastfed and one bottlefed. The story could show the difference in their health.

Have a discussion after the play. Let the audience ask questions and put their views. Try to lead the discussion so that the audience comes to some positive conclusion.

Roleplay can be used in a similar way, but is especially useful for training. For example, some trainees can act mothers with certain problems, such as "not enough milk". Others can practise counselling them. They can practise asking sensitive questions, and being supportive, before they give advice. Or trainees can roleplay how a mother-to-mother support group might work, or talking to difficult colleagues at work.

12.7 CODE OF MARKETING OF BREASTMILK SUBSTITUTES

For some time it has been recognized that the promotional activities of manufacturers of breastmilk substitutes (infant formula, proprietary cereals and other baby foods) encourage women to feed their babies artificially and to introduce cereal foods before the baby is 4 months of age.

The effect has been particularly serious in large towns, but it has spread to smaller towns and villages also.

Promotional activities include:
- Making attractive advertisements to use as posters in clinics and hospitals.
  These may show healthy babies and happy mothers, and suggest that good health is the result of feeding the baby their brand of formula.
- Giving calendars which advertise their product.
- Giving health workers free samples of infant food hoping that the health worker will use them and that mothers will copy the health worker.
- Giving free samples to mothers as they leave hospital after delivery.
  We know that these promotional activities and advertisements are

one of the factors that make women stop breastfeeding. Mothers are persuaded that breastmilk substitutes are as good as breastmilk, or better; or that their baby needs formula as well as breastmilk. Some families come to believe that they are not doing the best for their baby if they do not give formula. They discover the dangers and expense of this decision too late.

In 1981, the World Health Organization (WHO) drew up "The International Code of Marketing of Breastmilk Substitutes". This Code called upon all the manufacturers of infant formula and weaning foods to stop advertising and promoting their products in this dangerous way. WHO called upon all member nations to adopt the Code and to make its provisions law in their countries.

A number of other countries have now prepared their own codes based on the WHO code. In some countries these remain recommendations. In a few countries the Code has become law. In 1983, Kenya prepared its "Code for Marketing of Breastmilk Substitutes".

Figure 50. There should be no picture of a healthy baby on the label of a tin of formula.

The Code has been published by the Kenya Bureau of Standards and should be available from them. It is a detailed document but its main provisions are:
– There should be no advertising of breastmilk substitutes to the general public.
– There should be no promotional activities such as giving free samples to mothers or to staff in any health facility, and no posters or calendars should be given.
– The labels on tins of formula should contain the clear declaration that breastmilk is best for babies. There should be no picture of a healthy baby on the label.
– The instructions on the tin should be very clear and easy to follow.

Responsibility of health workers for the Code

Health workers are responsible for noticing any activities which go against the Code. They should forbid those activities that are in their power to forbid.

For example, health workers should:
❑ Remove any posters in their institution which advertise formula or baby cereal.
❑ Refuse to talk to representatives of the companies which manufacture baby foods.
❑ Refuse to accept free samples or other gifts.
❑ Refuse to allow representatives to give free samples to the mothers in their care.
❑ Make sure that anyone who gives a talk about cereal foods does not recommend them for babies under 4 months of age.

If health workers notice activities which they cannot themselves do anything about, they should report them to one of the following:
Kenya Bureau of Standards, P. O. Box 54974, Nairobi.
IBFAN Africa, P. O. Box 34308, Nairobi.
Breastfeeding Information Group, P. O. Box 59436, Nairobi.

Conclusion

Take every opportunity to explain to individuals, to groups, to the staff of health facilities, and to the media, about breastfeeding. Every time that you do this, someone will learn something, and gradually the message that breastfeeding is the only perfect way to feed a baby will spread.

Make sure that you set an example and breastfeed yourself; do *not* use a bottle. Make sure that people can see how you manage.

But remember that no amount of public education can help a new young mother who lacks confidence in herself, or whose baby is given prelacteal feeds in hospital. She needs skilled help, personal advice and friendly support, from the health workers who care for her, and from the community in which she lives. The health workers and counsellors who have special understanding and skills are most effective if they work with individual mothers, and if they help their colleagues to learn the same skills.

Index